STRESS-FREE MONEY

STRESS
FREE
MONEY

OVERCOME THESE *SEVEN OBSTACLES*
to FIND FINANCIAL FREEDOM

CHAD WILLARDSON, CRPC®, AWMA®
CREATOR OF THE FINANCIAL LIFE INSPECTION®

LIONCREST
PUBLISHING

STRESS-FREE MONEY
Overcome These Seven Obstacles to Find Financial Freedom

ISBN   978-1-5445-1673-8 *Hardcover*
      978-1-5445-1674-5 *Paperback*
      978-1-5445-1675-2 *Ebook*

*To my wife, Amber, who always believes in me and
supports me following lofty dreams and goals. She does
this despite my weaknesses, which she sees up close.*

*To my kids—McKinley, Pierce, Sterling, Bentley and
Beckham—who eagerly listen (most of the time) to my countless
teaching moments and lessons on financial success.*

*To my parents for raising me to believe that relationships
and life experiences are more important than money.*

To my colleagues and employees who have been on this journey with me.

*To my clients and friends who have entrusted me with their most
important goals and concerns, their fears, their aspirations, and
the stewardship of their money—all through thick and thin.*

CONTENTS

INTRODUCTION

It was Sunday, September 15, 2008. I was calmly sitting in the second row at church for the Sunday service. My wife, Amber, and our two little kids at the time, McKinley and Pierce sat next to me. The sermon that morning was on "finding hope in life's difficult trials."

Little did I know how badly I would need that message just a few short minutes later.

I glanced down at my phone to check the time, and noticed I had twenty-seven new texts and eleven missed calls. How was that possible? My heart dropped, and a million thoughts raced through my head.

What was going on?

Then, my phone started to ring again. I recognized the number: it was a very important client of mine. I'd never stepped out of church in the middle of the service, but I could tell I needed to this time; something was obviously wrong.

"I need to take this phone call," I whispered to my wife, tapping her gently on the shoulder. From the concerned look on my face and the abrupt manner in which I was getting up to leave, she could tell it was urgent.

I pushed answer on my phone and walked out to the foyer on the front right side of the chapel.

I tried to put on my calm voice, feeling totally unprepared to answer this phone call.

"Good Morning Mike, how are you?"

"How am I? Is my money all gone now? Have you seen the news? How could this possibly happen? Did you know about this? What does this mean for my money? Is it even going to be there tomorrow morning? I can't do this, Chad. I didn't sign up for this."

Immediately, I tried to calm Mike down and reassure him things would be okay, not fully understanding the root of his concern, but confident I would find the answers for him. While we were talking, I heard the text notifications buzzing repeatedly, and I saw that a colleague from the office was trying to call in. I calmly let Mike know that I would get more information and then call him back soon. I needed to pick up the other call before it went to my voicemail.

"Are you kidding me? This is unreal! They blew it! Almost one hundred years of history on Wall Street, flushed down the toilet because of greed and stupidity!"

"I've been in church this morning and haven't been following the news," I said to my colleague. "What exactly happened?"

"Merrill Lynch just almost went completely out of business and had to get bailed out. Bank of America bought it in some backroom deal. Supposedly by tomorrow morning, the bull would be dead."

A flood of stress and uncertainty welled up inside of me. How could we go from one of the historic investment firms on Wall Street with nearly one hundred years of a solid reputation to one begging for a buyout?

As I read through my texts, they were filled with more shock and more questions.

I didn't know what to think. Was I working for the bank now? More importantly, my mind raced to what it always does: the *people*. What did this mean for my clients? And their investment portfolios?

WHO AM I?

That fateful day when I stepped outside church was over a decade ago, at the time of this writing.

Things have changed since then.

Let's start, though, with one thing that hasn't changed—what attracted me to this business in the first place—helping people. I enjoy being the trusted advisor for families and businesses looking to achieve financial and life goals.

I put my skillset in personal finance and investing and my passion for helping people to work at Merrill Lynch early in my career. I spent nine years there and eventually ranked in the top 2 percent of 16,000 financial advisors nationally. While my career there blossomed, I felt more and more torn and conflicted. I saw the industry go through many changes, especially in 2007 through 2009, many of which were designed to protect the banks and the shareholder interests rather than the clients who entrusted us with their money. I'll share some of those with you later in this book. For now, it's important for you to understand that at that pivotal time in my life and career, I felt like my arms were being pulled in a tug-of-war: On one side, what was most important to my employer and the banks. On the other side, what was best for my clients.

I had to choose. And I chose the clients.

I left behind all the perks of Wall Street to become an entrepreneur, founding my company, Pacific Capital. Today, as a firm of independent fiduciaries, we have the freedom to use the resources and the research from the big companies without any pressure to sell their products or policies. We have no quotas. Our only obligation is to our clients, no strings attached. It's a great feeling to confidently look them in the eye and tell them how our recommendations are in their best interest. Furthermore, many of our clients are business owners themselves. Having taken that leap myself, I can confidently tell them that I understand all that comes with that, too.

At the end of the day, though, this book is *not* about Pacific Capital.

It's also *not* about me.

Instead, it's about how having an aligned, goal-focused financial strategy—which is possible, if you overcome the seven obstacles we'll cover in this book—can relieve stress and improve your life.

WHAT TO EXPECT IN THIS BOOK

Sadly, over 75 percent of Americans admit to experiencing a "high level of financial stress" in their life. Like it or not, money truly touches everything you do. You make money decisions every single day. In fact, financial stress is the number one cause of divorce in America.[1] It can also lead to the following: an increased risk of heart attack, obesity, accelerated hair loss, lack of sleep, diminished sex drive, depression, and more.

What are some of the reasons you feel stress about money? Maybe you feel like you haven't saved enough for your future. Maybe you're anxious about your investments and the markets. Maybe you're upset at all the money you see going to taxes

---

1 Welch, Stewart. "The #1 Reason for Divorce?" al.com, July 5, 2018, https://www.al.com/business/2018/07/the_1_reason_for_divorce.html.

and feel like you're missing out on opportunities to keep more of your hard-earned money. Maybe you can't stop worrying about when the next recession is coming. Maybe you wish you understood all of this better—for your personal finances *and* your business finances—but there's so much to learn and so many different opinions on the "right" thing to do with your money. Maybe you and your loved ones have completely different philosophies on saving and spending. Maybe one of you feels the burden of responsibility and the stresses that go with it, and the other seems to not care enough. (Because you're the one reading this book, I can already guess which one you are.)

Whatever the cause of your stress, I bet it's there. There's a level of anxiety nagging in the back of your mind because you know you need to improve some aspects of your financial life, but you aren't sure where to start or whom to trust, right?

I get it.

Our industry doesn't seem to help alleviate that stress. The Wall Street machine is intimidating, and it cashes in on the high emotions of fear or excitement you may feel at any given moment. You've also probably felt uneasy about financial advice you've received in the past, wondering if it was really best for you or more in favor of the person giving you the advice.

The list of reasons we feel stress about money is never ending. But there's good news: you don't have to feel this way anymore.

In this book, you will learn how to overcome the top seven obstacles to your financial freedom. You will see how to quickly remove the financial stress from your life, so you can instead spend your time and energy focusing on what you love.

This book will show you why you've got to break your addiction to the unhealthy financial fast food, starting today. You'll be able to easily spot if your financial advisor is working for you or against you, get a clearer picture of how investment fees are truly impacting you, and gain a better understanding of the risks you're taking with your money.

The days of feeling like your financial life is full of misfit puzzle pieces? The days of having no goal in mind and no complete picture of what your financial life should be? Those days are over.

Let's get started.

NO CLEAR GOALS

"You can't hit a target you cannot see, and you cannot see a target you do not have."

—ZIG ZIGLAR

Imagine walking into a medical office, filling out a few papers with some background information on yourself, and then being rushed back to see the doctor. After a few pleasantries, the doctor opens a cupboard, pulls out a big bottle of pills, and starts touting all the great effects the medicine could have on you. He highly recommends you start taking it and ditch your other prescriptions, because his other patients really like these new ones better. No thorough health exam, no detailed questioning or diagnostics, no overall health planning—just a recommendation for these specific pills he already had ready to sell on the shelf.

Feels dirty, doesn't it? Prescription without thorough diagnosis is malpractice. This scenario seems unthinkable in the medical field, yet most people experience just such a scenario when working with the 600,000+ "financial advisors" in the country. Most financial professionals sell one-size-fits-all investment pills instead of crafting a personalized financial strategy for individual clients.

GET A ROAD MAP

Just as your individual health conditions, family genes, and needs must be at the center of any valid, valuable health plan, your personal goals, concerns, and dreams must be at the core of your family's financial life blueprint.

Many people have investment accounts and a goal to someday retire. They want to make sure if something happens to them, their family will be taken care of. Their pain point, though, is that without having specific and clear goals, there's really no way to track or measure progress. Without that point of reference, too many people hand over their money to financial hucksters selling magic pills—or annuities, investment portfolios, and insurance policies as the case may be—without considering their overall context before taking action.

Couples often come into an initial appointment with many different financial statements in hand. We hear questions like this often—and maybe you've even asked them before: "Here's what we have. Can you help us? How can we do this better? How would you invest differently? Do you think we're getting a decent investment return from our current financial advisor? Are we paying too much? Do you think we have enough money to retire? Are we on track? How much do you think we need before we can finally stop working?"

In these situations, we have to start by taking a step back. We need to define their goals clearly before we can do any analysis. They have to know exactly what they're trying to accomplish before I—or anyone—can offer them relevant advice. I have found that most people haven't thought about their goals, or at least verbalized them, before coming to see us. Sometimes couples get a deer-in-the-headlights look and ask each other, "Well, what are *your* goals for retirement?" The two often have different ideas about what life should look like when they stop working or what their savings should be going towards.

Maybe coming up with a written plan seems like unnecessary or irrelevant work, but consider this: According to a study of Harvard MBAs, only 3 percent had clear, written goals and a plan to accomplish them. The result? Those in the 3 percent earned, on average, *ten times* more than the other 97 percent combined. If you knew you could give yourself a tenfold better chance of meeting your financial targets, I'm guessing your time planning and preparing would feel worth it.

GETTING SPECIFIC WITH YOUR GOALS

A lot of people come to us without a clear direction or sense of purpose. Planning for your financial future often doesn't seem fun; in fact, it feels overwhelming. You may feel uncertain regarding how to proceed or which options are available to you. It can be difficult or even counterintuitive to break your financial plans down into such specific, measurable goals. Spelling out your exact plans on paper can also feel stressful, because once you do so, you're more accountable.

Given the massive amount of financial information and advice available, from all kinds of advisors as well as online and in the news, you may feel confused or even paralyzed. You may not know what your goals should be. You're just trying to do the best you can with the money you're earning at the moment.

I get it. And it's my job to help.

To come up with a plan, we first need to get on the same page about your well-defined goals. These are *specific*. You need to be clear about what you want your money to do for you and for those you care about. For example, one couple we work with has a goal to take two big family trips a year, including one trip in which they pay for all the family members, spouses, and grandkids. Such a goal prompts follow-up questions. How much would such a vacation cost? If they have a family tradition of going to Hawaii, maybe that one family trip has a price tag of

$30,000. We can then incorporate that clear, specific goal with an accurate cost into their planning process.

Pro Tip: With each financial goal you decide on, add the phrase "so that..." to help determine the purpose behind your money and your goals.

Once you have a specific, tangible target, you will feel much more motivated to change your financial habits, because you have clarity and a sense of purpose. In the case of an annual trip to Hawaii, that couple wants to maintain a family tradition so that they can strengthen family bonds and make great memories with their grandkids. The cost of that personally meaningful goal is approximately $30,000 per year. Having a number to work toward to achieve it will help them exercise more discipline with their saving and spending. Working together toward that goal is a wholly different experience from simply handing an advisor some statements and asking, "Can we do better with different investments?"

Clients commonly start out with very vague, unmotivating goals. They want us to help them get a better return on their investments or earn a better interest rate. Whether we can achieve that result for them is actually irrelevant, because it's a bad idea to try to increase returns without a purpose. It's a slippery slope to have no context or goals for an investment portfolio. If you don't know how much money you need or how you want to use it, then you'll always be trying to make more, which can lead to taking on unnecessary risks.

If you simply assign your financial advisor to try and make you lots of money, you're essentially letting someone gamble with your nest egg. You will be more successful if you write down specific, meaningful goals, figure out how much they cost, the timeline of when you may need access to your money, and then work together to design the best strategy to fund your goals. We typically aim to help families create a list of at least five to seven financial priorities and understand the *why* for each of them. Then, we work backward to see how we can achieve them while taking on as little financial risk as possible.

The example of a particular family vacation is extremely clear and actionable. Some people start with a more vague notion, such as wanting to retire in ten years, but at least such a timeline offers more specificity than simply getting better returns. When people tell me they want to retire, we ask them when they'd like to switch from being dependent on a paycheck to paying bills via their investment income. They often don't know and ask us what a good age would be, but the answer really depends on how much they'll be spending. I've found it's better to decide *at what income level* you'd like to stop working rather than *at what age* you'd like to stop working. It comes down to this: to achieve success, you need to work in this order—know what you want to do, figure out how much it costs, and then plan to generate that income.

THE GOALS CONVERSATION®

Given how rarely people know exactly what they want from their finances—and given how important it is for us to be on the same page—the first meeting with the team at my firm is called the Goals Conversation. That conversation involves getting crystal clear on the outcomes you want, before discussing any specific actions to take with your money. Goals can involve all sorts of outcomes, not just retirement. The process requires finishing the sentence, "We want to pay for…so that…"

The Goals Conversation is specific to my company, but that doesn't mean its premise should be. In fact, its premise is relatively simple, and it shows a level of depth and care you should expect if you want to get the most out of your experience with your advisor (or preferably) fiduciary. To do your part, given the complexity of the issue, there are questions you should ask yourself—and that your financial professional can help you work through—when having these big picture goal conversations: What is important and unimportant to you? What keeps you up at night? What does money mean to you? What, if anything, do you want to pass on to the next generation?

Here's a great example: we just had a Goals Conversation with a couple who has four children. We asked whether they wanted to pay for the children's college. It turned out they weren't on the same page. The wife had paid her way through college without help from her parents, which taught her a sense of responsibility and self-reliance. She felt it was important to teach her kids to work hard and be financially invested in their education. The husband, on the other hand, cherished the experience of focusing on his studies without worry or the burden of student loans or part-time jobs after class, because his parents had paid his tuition in full. They were on completely different ends of the spectrum.

As we talked through the issue together, the pair agreed to pay for the freshman year of college for each of their children, up to a private-school level of tuition. They struck a balance between instilling a work ethic and supporting their children in a way that aligned with their values. Once they established the clear goal, they had to consider its significant cost and begin planning for it. Knowing exactly how much they'd cover for each child gave them a well-defined benchmark, whereas a goal of simply "helping my kids pay for college" would not offer a concrete number to save toward.

Another problem is that it's hard to cultivate a long-term mentality when you're lost in the present-moment noise. People just don't want to think about all the different areas of their financial life or know how to do so, and they end up winging it.

"In the absence of clearly-defined goals, we become strangely loyal to performing daily trivia until ultimately we become enslaved by it."

—ROBERT A. HEINLEIN

In your initial Goals Conversation, you should go through every aspect of your financial life. What worries or concerns you? What goals do you have for your family or your business? We ask a lot of open-ended questions in order to discover the underlying priorities. We also ask follow-up questions to dig deeper. If you want to retire at age fifty, which is relatively young, we'd certainly ask, "Why did you choose that age?" Maybe your dad died at fifty-two, and you don't want to work until you die. In that case, health concerns and an early retirement plan would become part of the financial planning process. We'd also find out what you want to enjoy doing in retirement and how you've prepared thus far.

Simply bringing in a pile of financial account statements and trying to make a better return represents a huge missed opportunity. There's so much more to understand and plan for in your financial life than can be captured by an arbitrary percentage return or nonspecific goal.

GOALS AS A MINDSET, NOT A TRANSACTION

Too often people approach a financial advisor with a transactional rather than goals-based mindset. For instance, a wealthy potential client once called us and said he had $1.5 million that he wanted us to invest. He was referred by a highly trusted friend of his and was ready to move the money over. On paper, he sounded like a great potential client. Most advisors would ask him to send over the paperwork to get started immediately. However, we wanted to first engage in a Goals Conversation and understand his situation better, and he had no interest. He didn't want to take the time or open up to us and instead just wanted a quick transaction.

In short, he wanted to do what is known in the industry as the "horse-race exercise:" he'd put some of his money with us and some of his money with someone else, then see who got him higher returns over a random short time frame, like six months or a year. I explained to him that our team has a different approach. We start with goals-based planning before giving any investment advice. Not only is that a better recipe for success, but as a fiduciary, that's our duty. That answer didn't satisfy him, so he upped the ante to three million.

"I appreciate your willingness to trust us with your money, but before we help manage any of your investments, we've got to understand your goals, your financial background, your investment time frame, and your purpose for the money," I explained.

Sounding shocked, he replied, "I don't really want to spend the time going through all that. C'mon, no advisor would turn down the chance to manage three million bucks—that's $30,000 to $40,000 a year of income for you! You sure about this?"

Ultimately, he accepted the fact that we weren't going to bend our principles, and he engaged with us to discuss his family's goals and has become a great client. It's tempting for both clients and advisors to take his initial approach: aim to make as much money as possible with as little conversation as possible. Such a transactional approach, which describes most of our industry, is quicker and easier in the short run—but failing to plan based on goals leads to problems down the road.

> All successful investing is goal-focused and planning-driven. All failed investing is market-focused and current-outlook-driven.

Most transactional advisors are brokers rather than fiduciaries. They get paid on commission, and they have quotas to meet. They're just trying to get their next promotion, reach a higher commission payout rate, or hit a specific commission level to get invited on an all-expenses paid trip. From their perspective, quicker is better. There's also a lot less work involved. It's not their fault, and I'm not saying they're bad people; that's just how our industry is.

As fiduciaries, we don't have the same short-term incentives. Goals-based planning takes longer and requires more effort on both sides, but it pays off in the long run. In order to get our clients somewhere meaningful, we—and they—have to know where they want to go. How can you plan your dream vacation if you don't have a destination in mind? Research shows that most people spend more time thinking about a one-week trip than they do about the thirty-year or 11,000-day journey we call retirement.

This concept is not foreign: I work with many wealthy, successful people. Success in anything—business, life—requires clear goals. That means that even if you're used to transactional relationships at work, you will also be able to see the value of goals-based planning, too. For example, you wouldn't open a business without first completing a business plan, right? When it comes to money, though, for some reason, people feel tempted to skip to the end rather than carefully planning their course. Every department in your business has clear goals and milestones to help track progress, so how could you skip that process in your own finances and expect to be successful?

DIY AT YOUR OWN RISK

Even financial professionals, if they're smart, recognize the value of getting neutral, expert advice.

For example, a successful insurance-based financial advisor with a seven-figure business income reached out to our team a few years ago about financial planning—even though he counsels clients on their retirement income and insurance policies for a living. At first, we were skeptical of his motives. We wondered what his angle was. Maybe he just wanted to come learn our process to implement in his own business? Turns out he was completely genuine. Even *he* recognized he needed professional, comprehensive, goals-based planning done by a fiduciary. It's gratifying to know that the clarity we encourage through our service can be valuable to a fellow professional in our industry.

You can certainly go through the process of determining your financial and life goals on your own. However, once you've got a basic idea of what you really want, there is great value in sitting down with a professional who does this every day. Speaking about your goals and concerns out loud helps you clarify the what and the why.

GET IT IN WRITING

By the end of this chapter, I hope you'll feel inspired to create a *written* financial blueprint for your family, starting with five to seven major financial goals. Every major decision going forward will relate back to how you will accomplish those goals. Your new blueprint then provides the road map for getting there. It's a summary of your strategy. By coming up with a financial success blueprint, you'll be among the elite 3 percent of people who have clearly written goals and an action plan.

> "Written goals have a way of transforming wishes into wants, cant's into cans, dreams into plans, and plans into reality. Don't just think it—ink it!"
>
> —DAN ZADRA

Once you have your clear, specific goals prioritized, you can work backward to determine your best course of action. Ask yourself, "What do I need to do in each area of my financial life to aim toward these goals?" Most investment accounts are not aiming at anything. They have no target, and you can't hit a target that doesn't exist.

Aiming for an arbitrarily higher return with no context represents the biggest mistake people make. Let's return to our example of the client who came to us with three million dollars and wanted the highest returns possible. Hypothetically, say he has a good year, and his portfolio goes up to $3.5 million. Say the next year, there's a huge recession, and the value drops to $2.5 million.

If he then decides it's time to retire, he'll need to start withdrawing money every month. Here's the problem: he didn't structure his portfolio with the goal of supporting his retirement beginning in two years. Instead, he took on a lot of risk to make as much money as possible, as if he had a much longer time horizon. In actuality, he's now hampered his quality of life in retirement. He'll have to sell investments when they're down, locking in losses, which will compound the declines in value.

As a result, he may have to scale back his lifestyle in retirement in order to avoid outliving his money. He didn't have an investment strategy to match his timeline and goals. In fact, he didn't articulate any goals. Instead, he just wanted to go for a short-term home run, and now he has to pay serious consequences.

This kind of scenario is exactly why I believe in setting goals before investing any money. Comprehensive, goals-based planning is the complete antithesis of just trying to beat the market and get the highest return possible. Rolling the dice and hoping everything goes well inevitably leads to mistakes.

Comprehensive, written plans help you not only get your money in order but also plan your future. Once you figure out what you want from life, you can manage your finances to help you get there. People tell us we're not just their financial planners, but also their marriage counselors and family life coaches. We help them uncover a meaning and purpose for their money, not just indiscriminately help them make more of it.

What's the point to simply saving money if you have no meaning or purpose behind it? Money is nothing more than a means to an end. You can't take it with you when you die. By engaging in deep reflection and goals-based planning, you can decide what your money—and your life—mean to you. Once you uncover that meaning, you can devote your energy to realizing your goals in a bigger and better way, because you'll have a clear direction.

In 2006, *USA Today* reported a study in which researchers selected a large number of people who made New Year's resolutions. They then divided the people into two groups: those who wrote their resolutions down, and those who had resolutions but did not write them down. The following year, they followed up with all of the study participants. The results were incredible. Of the people who had set resolutions but did not write them down, only 4 percent had actually followed through and achieved them. However, among the group who had written down their goals (average additional time taken was less than twenty minutes), 44 percent had followed through on them. As Brian Tracy states in his book *No Excuses*, "This is a difference of more than 1,100 percent in success, and it was achieved by the simple act of crystallizing the resolutions or goals on paper."[2]

---

2   Tracy, Brian. *No Excuses!: the Power of Self-Discipline*. Philadelphia, PA: Da Capo LifeLong, 2014.

If you write down that you want the freedom to travel with your spouse two months out of every year, you'll naturally have excitement and passion around that clear and specific goal. It carries so much more weight than the vague notion of "having enough money for retirement." Instead of leaving the future as a murky haze of not working, you can picture yourself backpacking through a different part of Europe every year starting at age fifty-five. See the difference?

It's also true that if you only have a general idea of what you want but no written strategy, you'll be much more tempted and distracted by all the financial noise in the world. You're more likely to make bad decisions in an emotional, transactional way. When you have no plan and no written strategy, and when your financial life isn't integrated, it's tempting to make one-off decisions. Such fragmented choices are often bad ones. Maybe you see something on the news, get excited about a company, and put money into it. The investment doesn't relate back to the overall plan. Instead, it's just speculation and gambling.

If you find yourself in front of someone trying to sell you a financial product but don't have a financial plan, you might be swayed by the sales pitch and sign on the dotted line, even if the product won't actually benefit you. On the other hand, if you know your goals, you can ask this professional how exactly the product would support those goals. If you don't get a convincing answer, you'll know to walk away.

A perfect example of this is when a highly educated, successful couple came to us with the goal of moving through our financial planning process. One of their considerations, in particular, stuck with me: they were about to put two life insurance policies in place, though they were merely a few years away from retiring and debt-free. Why? A family friend, who was also a life insurance agent, recommended they establish a financed policy where they would borrow $500,000 per year from a bank for ten years (yes, that's $5 million total borrowed) to add to their annual premium payments. The appeal of having a larger account value of cash and larger potential death benefit was enough for them to say, "I guess that sounds like a good idea."

It wasn't. These two policies would equate to over $10 million in life insurance and over $5,000,000 in debt to the bank, both of which seemed excessive and extremely unnecessary to our team. The couple felt some urgency from the agent to sign the documents and get the policies in place.

When we asked how this amount was decided upon or how the recommendation fit into their overall financial plan, they didn't have an answer. In our professional opinion, such a move would add significant cost and risk to their financial life. Not only that, but it didn't fit into the goals they'd expressed to us. Additionally, after further research by our team, we discovered that the agent's commissions on the deal were going to be over $300,000.

Thankfully, after going through a true financial planning process with our team, they understood what made the best financial sense for their family—and avoided a potential future train wreck.

A goals-based approach to financial planning serves as the backbone or framework to help you make decisions and ultimately reach your goals. Just the act of writing down your dreams and goals ignites an entirely new dimension of consciousness, ideas, and productivity to the powerhouse that is your subconscious mind.

PLANNING ESSENTIALS FOR ENTREPRENEURS

Well-thought-out, written plans are particularly important for small business owners, who have greater responsibility for long-term planning than the average employee and who face special financial considerations.

We work with many business owners and see two common mistakes among them all the time:

- Because of a fragmented financial life, they're often not taking full advantage of all the tax deductions available to them. Either they don't have a small business retirement plan set up, or they have one that isn't maximizing the opportunities available. They could be doing better for themselves and saving more in taxes.
- They take a suboptimal approach to paying themselves. So many small business owners are underpaying or overpaying themselves in wages, which affects their tax and financial planning outcomes.

They make these mistakes because they don't have a comprehensive, written plan integrating their personal financial life along with their business financial life. They don't have a fiduciary financial advisor helping them coordinate with their tax professional. If you don't have a clear plan developed, you'll simply turn in your information to the CPA every January and keep making the same mistakes year after year. If this is you, you may have a decent tax preparer but not an actual strategist or financial plan.[3]

> Ask yourself who is giving you strategic planning advice. If your only financial professional is a CPA who crunches numbers without discussion, then the answer is nobody.

There are many benefits people overlook because they treat their business money and planning as totally separate from their personal money and planning, when in reality the two are completely related. If you're the business owner, you are the business. Everything should be coordinated together instead of separated in little silos. It's important to optimize your outcomes and make win-win decisions that are good for the business and for you personally.

DITCH FRAGMENTATION

Too often, working with a CPA or considering tax concerns represents a fragment of financial life rather than a part of an integrated whole. If everything you've done with financial professionals up to this point is transactional, then you'll have no plan to refer back to. The temptation will be to evaluate every decision as a standalone transaction, when it's not.

---

3   Disclaimer: For tax advice specific to your situation, consult your tax professional, preferably one who engages in strategic planning and not just filing returns for you.

For example, say you're wondering if it's a good time to sell a big piece of real estate. Real estate prices are up, so you assume the answer is yes. However, if you sell it without looking at your overall integrated plan and considering how hefty capital gains might affect your tax bracket and retirement income, you might be in for an unpleasant surprise. Also, more important than whether you can make money on the deal is what you plan to *do* with the money afterward. Maybe you don't need that lump sum for anything in particular right now and it would be better to continue owning the property.

We had a client who faced that exact scenario of selling property prior to working with our team. They sold the property and reinvested the proceeds into a different property in an attempt to avoid hefty tax consequences. However, because he and his wife weren't working from a comprehensive plan at the time, when they later went to their financial advisor, they learned their transaction didn't qualify for the 1031 tax-free exchange they'd tried to do on the advice of a realtor. There was some complexity to the transaction because they sold raw land. And, unfortunately, they didn't have an advisor at the time helping to coordinate their overall strategy. The realtor wasn't a tax professional and just wanted to close the big sale. As a result, this couple got hit with a surprise tax bill for hundreds of thousands of dollars. As retirees on a fixed income, they were forced to raid their monthly income-producing investments, essentially making unanticipated fire sales in order to cover the unexpected tax bill. They came to us as a referral after having that upsetting, costly experience.

A fragmented financial life has other downsides as well. You'll end up with lower tiers of service and higher tiers of expenses. In other words, you will typically overpay and be underserved. If you have money, insurance policies, and investments all over the place in different hands, you're effectively a small client at each of them and will usually get less service and attention. If you had a single, consolidated plan, on the other hand, you'd get a higher level of service at a lower cost.

COORDINATING ALL THE MOVING PARTS

Not having an integrated plan leads to many unintended consequences. A good financial plan must include coordination among professionals on your behalf and regular, proactive communication. If you want to be involved in the conversation, then by all means get involved. If you trust your team to handle the logistics and give you recommendations during your strategy sessions, that's fine, too. One way or another, though, all the pieces of your financial life have to work together rather than in silos.

A financial advisor can help develop the plan and coordinate the professionals involved, such as lawyers, insurance agents, CPAs, and so on. An advisor doesn't replace those professionals but rather keeps the whole team aligned with your overall goals. Coordinating and communicating is key; a good advisor will be in ongoing conversation with all the professionals who impact your finances (with your permission, of course). I strongly believe your advisor and CPA should talk at least twice a year on your behalf, though in my experience, that coordination is extremely rare.

Another benefit of coordinating moving parts is that everyone is aware of life changes. When these changes happen, there are legal documents and various forms that need updating. If they're not, there will be major consequences. I remember when a colleague back at Merrill Lynch had a situation in which a high-income client of theirs was married for just two years in his early twenties, got divorced, and then later married someone else for over twenty-five years. He and his second wife built a great life and had four children before he unexpectedly passed away in his mid-fifties, while three of their kids were in college. They were in a very expensive phase of life. His $3.5 million life insurance policy went to his ex-wife whom he hadn't seen in over twenty-five years—all because he hadn't updated the beneficiary forms. It was devastating to his widow and children. This tragedy was the result of a fragmented financial life and the lack of a trusted financial coach in charge to help coordinate all the different professionals and moving parts.

Life insurance can be an Achilles heel in another way, too, if not everything is coordinated. Another common example of this comes from a client who had four different life insurance policies when he started with us, all for different amounts and all requiring monthly or quarterly premium payments. He said he wasn't sure why he had them all—they'd just been recommended by his friend, who was his insurance agent.

Together, he was paying $3,000 per month—that's $36,000 a year—for life insurance, and he couldn't even articulate why. Such a number might be higher than average, but the general situation of having unnecessary or redundant policies is quite common. By evaluating his specific circumstances and considering his health, we were able to help him consolidate into a single policy with a higher death benefit (than all of the four policies combined) without having to pay any more premiums going forward, a net cash flow benefit of $36,000 per year.

WAKEUP CALLS

Sometimes, we get a wakeup call regarding our own financial fragmentation. I once was introduced to a couple that was preparing to go on a month-long European vacation in celebration of their recent retirement. This big trip had been in the works for many years, and they'd planned and mapped out all the different destinations they wanted to visit. Every day was carefully planned. You can probably guess what unfortunately had *not* been carefully planned: their financial life. The big trip outside of the United States suddenly made them worry about what their adult children would do if something happened to them while away. The kids and grandkids wouldn't have any clue where to start, what to do, or whom to call. This couple had fourteen financial accounts at eight different banks and investment firms and six insurance policies with four different insurance companies.

Preparing for the trip made them realize they'd leave behind a big mess if anything happened to them.

This couple is not alone in being complacent until an external circumstance instigated a sense of urgency inside of them. In their case it was a big dream vacation, whereas others don't get their ducks in a row until they're about to sell their business, a family member passes away, a family member gets divorced, someone needs to move into assisted living, and so on.

We find many of our clients become caretakers for their parents, which can also be a wakeup call. The confusion and stress of going through their parents' bills and documents makes them realize the consequences of disorganized financial fragmentation. They need to address the expense of long-term care for their loved ones and don't know where that income should come from. They don't know which life insurance policies exist or which plans are still in place, if any. They don't know if they need to sell the home to pay for the cost. In such cases, it's hard to make financial decisions without an overarching blueprint to refer to and someone in charge of coordinating all the moving parts.

Watching the experience of parents can be a motivator to get your own financial life in order. If you were in the same situation, who would your kids call? Do you have anything written down and in place for your family to refer to? It's very important to have a written plan in place so that your family knows your goals and intentions as well as where the money is to pay for everything.

> One way to remove your stress about money is knowing your family will be well taken care of in a crisis.

Other wakeup calls might not come from difficult emotional times, but they can still have huge financial implications. For example, no one wants to overpay in taxes—it's much better to plan now rather than finding that motivation later because you've lost unnecessary money to the IRS. We often work with people who have overpaid in the past, because they didn't have good coordination between their financial and tax advisors. Because they didn't have clear goals, they left money on the table for years.

The longer you wait to address all the pieces, the harder it is to achieve the outcomes you want. Essentially, if your life is financially fragmented and you don't know your cash flow numbers, you're operating in the dark.

If you haven't had a wakeup call yet, I encourage you to let this be yours.

TOO MUCH IS NOT ALWAYS A GOOD THING

Sometimes, financial fragmentation leads to overconcentration in particular areas. If you have three financial advisors or brokerage firms, it's a little bit like having three doctors. You might end up getting prescriptions for ibuprofen from all of them, but each might not realize the others have also prescribed ibuprofen. If you take all the ibuprofen they've each prescribed, you could overdose.

Each of the doctors in this example *think* they're giving you the dose you need, but they aren't taking the other doctors into account. Similarly, all your financial advisors could expose you to a certain segment of the market that would make sense as part of a comprehensive plan but becomes too risky and overloaded in a fragmented situation. In short, if you think you're being smart with your money by talking to a lot of different professionals, you can actually end up with a lack of diversification, more risk, and worse results.

By the same token, it's not safe to take certain medications together—doing so can make you sicker or even kill you. It's the same here: investing in every possible opportunity under the sun recommended by a slew of different advisors who aren't talking to each other isn't necessarily less risky—it may actually be more so.

> If you think because you get statements from Wells Fargo, Bank of America, JP Morgan, and Morgan Stanley, that means you're diversified—think again. We call this brick-and-mortar diversification. You've successfully diversified where your mail comes from, but not necessarily where you are invested.

When we see people who are deep into brick-and-mortar diversification, we often look at the actual holdings on those statements and find each one has the same securities or own the same funds with overlapping investments inside of them. Buying the same thing in three places isn't diversification. If, for example, you're overconcentrated in technology funds, you're actually in a very high-risk position despite working with different brokers. If the technology sector dips next year, you'll lose a lot more money than if you'd truly diversified with a single coordinating advisory team working toward clearly identified goals.

Having a single team working on a coherent plan brings confidence to make financial decisions, even if you never face a crisis. Knowing what do to, how to do it, and why with regard to your finances brings tremendous peace of mind. You'll have more clarity, less stress, and lower anxiety. Your financial advisory team should be transparent with their recommendations by tying them back to your goals and sharing the pros and cons of each piece of advice. Your team will know you and your family intimately and will be there to guide you through every big decision.

> Once you have clear goals and a trusted team helping you, you're well on your way toward that stress-free mindset.

LACKING A PLAN IS EXPENSIVE

The missed opportunities resulting from financial fragmentation and lack of planning have substantial costs.

For example, I met an attorney who once worked at a large law firm and was making around $400,000 a year. She decided she wanted to be her own boss and start her own firm. She left the corporate world and set up shop. Unfortunately, she didn't make money for the first two years because of the startup expenses and challenges rebuilding a clientele, nor did she do any strategic tax planning around that situation. When she finally came in to see her financial advisor (about five years after leaving the corporate law firm), she learned she'd missed a great opportunity to save on taxes.[4]

She could have converted her large individual retirement accounts to a Roth during those two years she had no income. She could have paid taxes while in a very low tax bracket and converted that money into tax-free investments that would have lasted the next forty years, then passed it on to her kids tax-free.

She only had a two-year window in her whole career where she essentially had no income, which would have been the perfect time to take advantage of this opportunity. However, she missed the opportunity, costing her hundreds of thousands of dollars in long-term tax differences—all because she had no integrated plan or strategy. If she'd had a cohesive plan and a coordinated team, she could have ensured the ability to retire with a much higher income and kept more of her hard-earned money.

Another example of how expensive the lack of planning can be comes not from someone starting out in their business, but from an older couple who owned a very significant Southern California rental real estate business before they sold it and retired. Their previous advisors were very transactional and did not have an integrated strategy tying each element of their portfolio back to their personal goals. Every time the firm or one of its advisors

---

4   Consult your tax professional for specific advice related to your financial situation.

had an idea, they made a sales pitch—which resulted in these clients having an inappropriately high-risk financial profile. Of course, the fees and commissions on these pitched ideas were extremely high for the financial professionals involved.

When we met the couple, we found their aggressive investment strategies were more appropriate for someone thirty-five years old than this couple in their seventies. Their goal was to produce steady and protected income, but their investments didn't align with that goal. Instead, they had many high-risk holdings that did not produce much income. They also had a lot of international and small-company penny stocks, and they'd bought into private real estate deals of foreclosures and distressed private businesses. This bad combination led to significant stress when the markets were volatile or deals didn't pan out.

Their previous advisors had pitched everything as having very secure high return, but some of the investments went bankrupt. The clients were retirees relying on bad professional advice, saying yes to each pitch without having a larger blueprint to reference. Their deliberation essentially amounted to something like, "I think that sounds like a good idea and will make us a lot of money, so let's give it a try." Naming the goal and having a written plan makes you less likely to react to ups and downs in the market. If you are working toward a goal, not chasing returns, emotional decision-making is reduced.

The bottom line? Making individual decisions on the fly might take less effort over the short run than taking the time to come up with a comprehensive, goals-based plan, but it is also costly and leads to big mistakes.

HAVING A PLAN REDUCES STRESS

Think, for a minute, about a surgeon. If they're going to operate on your foot, why do they check your blood pressure and all your other vital signs before surgery? Because you can't just operate on the foot and ignore the rest of the body—you've got to know how the whole system is working.

If you find a good surgeon who can assess how the whole system is working and come up with an appropriate treatment, you'll feel better about moving forward with the surgery. Whatever's been ailing you can heal. On the other hand, if you find someone who's just in a rush to sell you on the most expensive procedure possible, you're in trouble.

The same is true for good financial advice. An experienced, independent fiduciary can help get a deep, complete picture of not only your current financial situation but also what you want to do with your money over the course of your life. Then, the two of you can work together to achieve that outcome. Just like getting a good health tune-up, getting your financial health under control can make you physically feel better, devote less time to worrying, and get the most out of your money and your life.

KEY TAKEAWAYS

- You are not alone if you've got a fragmented financial life, but now is the time to take action.
- It's worth the time and effort required to put the pieces together and figure out your core goals, which will then drive all your financial decisions going forward.
- It's essential to coordinate your financial decisions if you want to achieve success, and real success requires a thoughtful, *written* plan.

FINANCIAL FAST FOOD

"The idea that a bell rings to signal when to get into or out of the stock market is simply not credible. After nearly fifty years in this business, I don't know anybody who has done it successfully and consistently. I don't even know anybody who knows anybody who has."

—JACK BOGLE, FOUNDER OF VANGUARD

It's 6:32 a.m. on a Tuesday morning, yet the headline article on CNBC is already describing the day in the markets: "The markets were up today based on increased optimism that a trade deal with China...*blah blah blah.*"

Let's think about this situation: at that point, the markets had literally been open for an entire two minutes! Did we really need an article describing the entire day's events, how much the market moved, and why, as if the day were already over? How would this information help you?

Let's look at this another way: you've probably been on a flight before when you experienced some real turbulence. Your seat started shaking a bit, but the flight attendants seemed to be calm at first. They were still walking the aisles and pouring drinks, so you figured it wasn't a big deal. What about when the pilot got on the intercom and told the flight attendants to quickly take their seats and buckle up? How did that feel?

That's the look I see on many people's faces when they first come into my office. They've got some unsettled anxiety about their financial life. It's my job and my privilege to help them breathe a little easier. That starts with ignoring the financial fast food.

> Fast food is popular because it's convenient, it's cheap, and the taste can be addicting. But the real cost of eating fast food never appears on the menu.

SOME THINGS NEVER CHANGE

In the early years of my career at Merrill Lynch, I conducted many dinner seminars here in Orange County, California. One of the first slides on the presentation was titled "Some Things Never Change," and it included a variety of past *TIME* magazine covers.

Each headline and picture showed a bold statement provoking significant fear in the minds and hearts of the readers at the time, including "1958: The Recession: How Deep? How Long?" and "1987: After a wild week on Wall Street, the world is different." My purpose in showing these old magazine covers was to help the audience see how silly the alarming headlines look in hindsight, now that we can examine the longer-term context of the claims. I say some things never change, because you'll probably notice the same topics dominating the news thirty to sixty years ago still dominate today.

> Make no mistake: the financial entertainment news media is your enemy, not your friend. If you let it, such media will distract you from your goals and destroy your ability to differentiate what is important from what is not.

I think of such news as "financial fast food." It's unhealthy and destructive—and the most dangerous part? It's very addictive.

You may already have alert notifications set up on your phone to help you feel like you're staying "informed," but does the financial entertainment news know what your personal long-term goals are? Is the investment advice or general financial guidance based specifically on your circumstances? Of course not. And by the way, it's worth saying that you have no recourse to the TV studio or article author if their recommendations don't work out for you.

We are all living through the exact content of this chapter today. I am editing the final draft of this book right now (March 2020) during a stay-at-home lockdown in the midst of the COVID-19 health pandemic. Tragically, many people have lost their lives and their jobs during this trying time. Hopefully, by the time you read this book, we have both survived and the panic regarding this virus is no longer dominating the thoughts and news headlines across the globe. In the previous four weeks, so many records have been broken in the financial markets. Panic and volatility (as measured by VIX) reached all-time highs, worse than the Great Depression, Black Monday in 1987, the tech bubble, September 11 and the Great Recession caused by subprime loans in 2007–2009.

Many believe that the reason the markets dropped so quickly and so frantically this month is because of the instant nature of news media consumption. The frightening news headlines are compounded with an estimated three billion people on social media every day and the panic spreads faster than ever before. The news anchors are looking for the most extreme and drastic pictures or videos available for their stories.

You need only to examine the incentives involved to see why it works this way: the shows and online media make profits based on viewers. They need your attention to make money, and they only get your attention with extremely dramatic stories! Watching just one segment is enough to scramble your brain, with all the different bits of information popping up and scrolling across the screen while someone yells at you to buy something, sell something, or provides new reasons to panic.

INSTANT GRATIFICATION

Steve Selengut, author of *The Brainwashing of the American Investor*, writes:

> Investors in general behave a lot like teenagers. They think that they know everything by listening to a stock market analyst; expect instant gratification; take unnecessary risks; fall in love too easily; ignore the voice of experience; prefer the easy (passive) approach; and feel that the lessons of the past don't apply to what's going on now. Duh, dude!

Because of this penchant among viewers for drama and instant gratification, the financial entertainment industry isn't so keen on stories of people who've made sound financial decisions and retired comfortably, on time, or early. Those stories don't sell magazines or have a high click-through rate. If they showed clips of everyday people making prudent financial decisions and avoiding the hype, very few people would watch or stay tuned. Producers are paid to stoke high emotions of either greed or fear, neither of which will help you make wise financial decisions.

Such financial fast food is hard to escape. In the early stages of this book, I was in Austin, Texas, for a meeting with my publishing team. It was an intense day of focus, as I spent around ten hours writing notes about how to help you, the reader, remove your stress about money and improve your progress toward personal financial freedom. I decided to book a massage at the spa in my hotel at the end of the day. The attendant guided me through the tour of the sauna with eucalyptus, the jacuzzi, and beautifully decorated locker rooms, finishing by showing me the door to enter the "relaxation lounge," which is the final space to decompress and wait for the massage therapist.

I looked forward to relaxing and detaching from the world for the next ninety minutes. You can imagine my shock, then, when I entered the "relaxation lounge" and found the big-screen TV blaring CNBC, with Jim Cramer yelling at the camera to buy and sell certain stocks. Oh, the irony. How could somebody possibly believe the relaxation lounge needed a TV, especially one showing CNBC financial entertainment news on high volume? Part of me thought I was being pranked, and I looked around the room for hidden cameras. Needless to say, after a real laugh out loud, I walked up to the set and turned it off.

If we don't turn off the TV and navigate away from the financial news sites, we're very likely to get caught up in the fear or greed and emotional hype of the day. The talking heads and so-called experts would have you believe you'd better pay very close attention, because they've got a crystal ball no one else has access to. Believing they can somehow predict the future may cause you to question your financial plan and long-term investment strategy. You'll start worrying you've made bad decisions, or you may feel FOMO tugging at you to buy the next IPO or "investment of the day" being hyped in the media. Whether driven by fear or by greed, letting emotions cloud your investment strategy is a clear recipe for failure.

> "Individuals who cannot master their emotions are ill-suited to profit from the investment process."
>
> —BENJAMIN GRAHAM (KNOWN AS THE FATHER OF MODERN PORTFOLIO THEORY)

It's a process, though. I get it: you almost can't escape the hype. Not paying attention to it takes real effort and discipline. Hopefully, by the end of this chapter, you'll see why that effort is worth it—and a key on your journey to stress-free money.

BASELESS PREDICTIONS

Not only is financial news all over your smartphone, but it comes through social media posts, blogs, emailed newsletters, and on the covers of business magazines proudly forecasting "the eight funds you must buy this year!" or the "ten stocks you don't want to miss!" How do those predictions actually work out, though? Who evaluates the past recommendations when they're publishing a new list every month, every year, or on some financial TV shows, *every single day*? Who wants to miss out on a big winner and be stuck on the outside looking in? Nobody, of course.

In point of fact, though, these predictions are based on nothing and don't yield results. For instance, consider a *TIME* magazine cover from March 2009. It shows a pair of hands gripping a fraying rope, with the headline "Holding on for Dear Life: The Economy and You."[5] The point of the issue was the death of stocks and how it was a terrible time to invest. The truth, though, was just the opposite. If you'd ignored the financial fast food and instead invested money back then, you would have realized more than a 500 percent return as of this writing,[6] based on the S&P 500, quintupling your money.

> Technology is incredible, but the information overload has made most of us worse at making financial decisions.

It's not uncommon for a client or potential client to come to me with some of these thoughts:

---

5   "The TIME Magazine Vault." 2020. *Time*. Accessed March 4, https://time.com/vault/year/2009/.

6   Current as of this writing, 2/12/2020.

"I just heard an economic recession is likely going to happen next month, so maybe we should consider selling our investments right before it happens."

"My CPA told me interest rates are going to go up a lot next quarter and housing prices will also be going up at least 10 percent for the rest of the year, so we should buy the other house right away."

Beware of fake financial fortune tellers. All of these are symptoms of "it's easy to predict what's about to happen" or the "next-shiny-thing" syndrome—the best evidence of which may be bitcoin. Not too long ago, the media obsession with bitcoin and cryptocurrency in general hit a peak. The infatuation was so intense that everyone was talking about it nonstop. The financial news was hyper-obsessed with the price of bitcoin, and hundreds of articles, social media posts, and blogs were being published and shared every day on the topic. Some personal friends of mine, who usually never talk about investing, began downloading apps to day trade the digital coins. They began texting me screenshots of the short-term hour-by-hour gains in their coin accounts.

For two consecutive months, in nearly every conversation, someone would ask me what I thought about bitcoin, how high I thought it was going to go, etc. One night, while at a friend's birthday party, I heard his son, a young high school student, excitedly and confidently telling some of us that Bitcoin was supposed to reach $100,000 per coin by the end of that year. He'd read it online, so it must be true, right?

Wrong!

The excitement and hype perpetuated by the news media are both addicting and harmful to your financial health. That's why I call it "financial fast food." Once the addiction to financial news traps you, it's hard to extricate yourself. Some of the friends who got addicted to the bitcoin hype were spending ten or more hours per day reading about the coins, tracking their trades, and texting each other how much money they were forecasted to earn. It completely distracted them from quality time with their family and productive time at work.

All that distraction was for nothing, because they didn't actually get rich quick. At the peak of the hype before Christmas in 2017, bitcoin reached $19,650. Maybe by the time you read this book, bitcoin will be well over $100,000 and this entire paragraph will look like silly advice. However, today it sits at a lowly value of $5,024.[7] All of the time, energy, and money invested in the media-hyped fad of the day did not yield positive outcomes for most people who got caught up in it.

EMOTIONAL INTELLIGENCE

One of the great transformations to see in a person's financial life is when they finally break free from the addiction to checking the markets daily and getting caught up in the headline clickbait alerts from the financial media. Instead of letting their emotions ride roughshod, they follow their values and goals-based, rational, long-term financial blueprint. Doing so represents financial intelligence and maturity.

7   2020. *Google Search*. Google. Accessed March 16, https://www.google.com/
     search?client=firefox-b-1-d&q=value+of+bitcoin.

> "In the world of money and investing, you must learn to control your emotions. High emotions equal low intelligence."
>
> —ROBERT KIYOSAKI, BESTSELLING AUTHOR
> OF THE *RICH DAD, POOR DAD* SERIES

I've had many people tell me something like the following once they've stopped trying to follow every shift in the market: "I don't even worry about it anymore. It feels like such a relief not to be attached to the fear mongering. My anxiety about the economy is down, and I'm more focused on what I can do to help my financial plan become a success."

Managing your emotions and exercising patience is crucial to your long-term financial success. One of the greatest threats to that success is getting caught up in issues you can't control or influence. Most often, the financial news media triggers the ideas and emotions that will push you off your path to success, either directly or through what you hear from friends and colleagues. When stock prices falter, the resulting steady drumbeat of negative news reports can drive many people to flee the markets out of fear (and miss out on potential gains as financial markets regain their strength). Deciding what and who will be your primary sources of financial advice and guidance will have a major impact on your success.

Between February 20, 2020 and March 23, 2020, the stock markets dropped approximately 38 percent. This was the fastest decline of 30 percent in history. I've never had more calls, texts, emails, and direct messages asking what could be done than I did during that time. These came from extended family members, friends, acquaintances, and people I'm connected to on social media. The panic and sense of extreme capitulation was very real for so many of these people.

When asked to share some advice and guidance during the crisis, I focused on a few main points. These are relevant now, and they'll be relevant later: On the scale of best to worst during extreme times, there are three routes you can take. Here they are, from worst- to best-case scenario.

- Worst-case: Throw in the towel, sell your investments, and abandon your financial plan.
- Middle-ground: Wait it out. Don't make big, permanent financial decisions. (If you do, you are likely to see what would have been temporary declines turn into permanent losses.)
- Best-case: Be opportunistic. Everyone talks about "buying low and selling high," but when it comes time to actually put this into practice, some become paralyzed by fear. Trust your advisor to make those moves on your behalf, putting you closer to reaching your personal and financial goals at a time when other investors are spinning out of control.

Through it all, we communicated proactively to our clients, helping them to stay calm, and leading with discipline and strategy. No matter what crisis we may face in the future, you should expect the same from your trusted fiduciary advisor.

WHAT *CAN* YOU CONTROL?

When I counsel my clients to tune out financial fast food, I'm not saying they should avoid being informed altogether. However, following a goals-based, well-informed plan means focusing on and getting informed about what you can control and ignoring things you can't. I don't believe staying up to date on the financial news helps your financial planning at all. You can't influence the forces covered by the news, and most of that information won't impact you, either. The news mostly represents static and noise.

INVESTMENT STRATEGY
SAVINGS VS. SPENDING
**THINGS YOU HAVE
TOTAL CONTROL OF**

YOU

HOW LONG YOU LIVE
WORKING INCOME
**THINGS YOU HAVE
SOME CONTROL OF**

TAX LAWS/REGULATIONS/POLICIES
MARKET RETURNS
**THINGS YOU HAVE
NO CONTROL OF**

However, you *can* influence your income and savings. You *can* control your choice of investment mix, retirement age, and tax planning. You *can* decide when to claim Social Security benefits and how to set up insurance protections for your family and assets. Estate planning is under your control, and you can decide how to prepare for all the what-if scenarios. What if there's death, divorce, disability, marriage, or a job change?

In all those arenas, staying up to date with the opportunities for your own financial planning is extremely important. Tax laws, personal goals, and family situations all change over time.

We typically see major life changes every five to eight years, and it's important to prepare for those. As a result, I recommend staying up to date with your own goals-based plan. Let the media continue to frustrate and confuse everyone else while you focus on what you can control in your own life.

LEAVE THE PROFESSIONAL WORK TO THE PROFESSIONALS

The only people who might benefit from paying close attention to the financial news are impartial financial analysts and fiduciary advisors. They can look at the information and determine relevant patterns for their clients. Because they aren't reacting emotionally, they can sift through the noise objectively to find any relevant information for your benefit. They have a clear process and set of guidelines in place to prevent hasty or reactive decisions in their firm.

That means a good advisor is worth listening to, just like having a skilled personal trainer for your finances. You can sit down with them every few months, talk about how you're progressing toward your goals, adjust accordingly, and stay focused on what you can control.

My firm employs a skilled technical analyst who follows such guidelines, and it's his job to relay what we need to know and how the data impacts what we are doing for clients in their financial strategies. As professionals entrusted to help people succeed, we maintain steady discipline and avoid getting emotionally caught up in the daily market hysteria. Sometimes, I think my lack of moment-to-moment reactivity surprises our clients. They'll ask me how the markets did today, and sometimes I can honestly tell them I have no idea. Chasing daily noise doesn't help me help them, so it's not worth my constant focus—or theirs.

TUNE OUT AND BREATHE EASIER

Getting off the treadmill of chasing the latest financial news can offer significant stress relief, freeing up mental space for pursuing your real goals. Having a financial plan doesn't just help the bottom line, but it can truly change your day-to-day experience of life.

We have a client in the commercial real estate business whose company placed multiple flat-screen TVs in the lobby blasting CNBC and other financial news all day long. Back in the day, this client would often read financial articles or pause in the lobby to see what the talking heads were excited about, leading him to constantly question his own strategy. He'd log in every couple of hours to check the fluctuations in his account, as the daily market news caused him anxiety and worry.

To me, keeping such close tabs on an account's fluctuating value is a red flag. If your goal this year is to improve your overall health, you don't step on the scale twenty times a day. Every time you eat, drink, sleep, or exercise, your weight will fluctuate a few ounces, but those minor, short-term fluctuations don't tell you anything about whether your overall diet and fitness plan is working. If you have a good weight-loss plan in place, you can see over the course of six months to a year that you've gone from 200 to 180 pounds, which is the relevant trend and progress worth measuring. The same applies to financial life goals.

Another way to think about the pointlessness of constantly tracking your portfolio movements is with the analogy of your home value. Would you get your house appraised every day of the year? Or multiple times throughout the day? Of course not—that's ridiculous. You're not moving houses every day, so why would you need that information? This is why many realtors would argue services like Zillow are essentially real estate fast food, churning out largely meaningless monthly or quarterly numbers that people obsess over. The financial news reporting is even worse, churning out numbers and values every second. You don't need second-by-second information about your financial portfolio any more than you need day-by-day appraisals of your house. You're not moving out of your financial plan every second, so the only relevant question is how the long-term trend matches up with your time horizon and goals.

With those facts in mind, over time, we helped our client put together a clear, long-term strategy. He learned how to sift through what matters and recognize what was just noise. He could then focus on progress and results rather than the hype in the financial news. Seeing the progress gave him confidence in what we were doing. Because the plan was working, he started to realize the day-to-day news didn't matter. Finally, he stopped hyper-checking the fluctuations in his accounts. He never completely stopped paying attention, but he loosened up as he realized he had a solid plan in place. Just recently he told me he felt healthier and calmer as a result. He has less anxiety and stress, and he can focus more on what he loves, primarily traveling with his family and golfing with friends.

Similarly, I've seen married couples hug at the end of meetings with us because they feel relieved from so much financial worry and uncertainty. They feel a burden has lifted, and they have greater confidence in the future, which impacts how they relate to each other. They understand what they're doing and why they're doing it.

> We've known clients who were so stressed over every little fluctuation in their portfolio and the news that they actually had heart attacks or strokes. Tuning all that out can bring real relief and can actually help your mental and physical health.

Such peace of mind—or lack of it—has real-world implications. Once, a woman told me that she believes her financial anxiety was the cause of her husband's heart attack, and she wanted to take his phone away. He literally tied his mood to how his investments did each day. People become addicted to watching every little move because it gives them a false sense of control. The more they watch and read, the more they think they can somehow control the outcomes, which is a total illusion. You can break free of the illusion and not only feel better in the moment but also achieve better long-term financial results than the people still stuck on the financial fast food treadmill.

KEY TAKEAWAYS

- Ignore the financial news media, and don't log in to your investment account every day.
- Consider the source: blanket, sensational, unaccountable advice isn't worth listening to, while personalized, impartial, accountable advice is.
- Focus on what you can control.

OBSTACLE 3

FOCUSING ON THE WRONG NUMBER

"Most people spend their whole lives climbing the ladder of success only to realize, when they get to the top, the ladder has been leaning against the wrong wall."

—STEPHEN COVEY

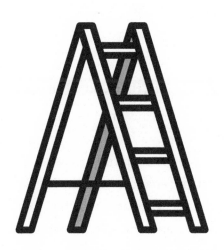

Recent studies indicate a majority of Americans have no idea how much they need to save for retirement, so they pick an arbitrary, round number like $1 million or $5 million. While having a random savings goal is obviously better than no goal at all, finding a more accurate retirement number doesn't have to be complicated. In this chapter, I'll cover questions you should ask yourself in order to determine what your actual number should be.

Besides that round number, people who study personal finance can sometimes think the number they're striving for is the investment return—in other words, the growth they need each year, such as 8 percent annually.

I'd like to bust the myth and say both of those numbers are wrong. Forget focusing solely on your calendar year rate of return. Forget your big lump sum, like it's some treasure you need at the end of the rainbow allowing you to retire into the sunset. Scrap all of that. The most important number you must be focused on is the monthly incoming cash flow you need to be comfortable.

DO YOU KNOW HOW MUCH YOU'RE SPENDING?

Finding your number means first looking at your spending. We often ask clients to look at their last twelve months of spending from their bank account, to start. Most banks will easily produce a report categorizing spending for the last year. (Note: Some people like to use the Mint app, which is free and very useful for tracking budget and spending information.) Whichever method you choose, use concrete data over a one-year period.

That allows you to calculate a meaningful average that includes major once-yearly expenses, such as property taxes, insurance, and so on.

Inevitably, everyone I've ever met underestimates their spending. It is shocking. Couples will tell me they think they spend around $11,000 per month, but when they run the numbers, it's actually closer to $15,000. Being off by $48,000 a year makes a big difference when you're forming a strategy to fund a thirty-year retirement. There are many miscellaneous expenses people don't account for, so don't guesstimate on this step.

> Finding the real number requires you to dig into your past in order to make the most accurate possible estimate for the future, including the expenses you have today that you won't have later and vice versa.

Here's a practical example: today, you might be paying for your kids to play travel sports and making a hefty mortgage payment every month. Your grocery bill when your kids are living at home in your forties is higher than when they've moved out of the house in your seventies. However, you might do more traveling and enjoy more expensive leisure activities in your seventies than you do today. Healthcare will also cost a lot more later in life. If you have more time in retirement to golf, eat out, and go to shows, those costs will go up.

The conventional wisdom estimates you'll spend 80 percent of your pre-retirement income once you stop working. In general, however, I find people typically fill up their spending to match what they're used to, even if the spending categories shift over time. Looking back twelve months will give you a clear picture of what you're truly spending. If you're comfortable spending that amount, it probably won't drop drastically even when you've paid off your mortgage and your kids have moved out. Your lifestyle expenses will just shift to other categories, such as healthcare and entertainment. In other words, you don't magically get a huge boost in disposable income once you retire.

THE PROBLEM ISN'T WHAT YOU THINK

An example of the importance of cash flow comes from a former financial planning client. The couple came to us making more than $300,000 a year. Their kids were in extremely expensive, well-known private schools. It cost $1,200 a month for the four- and seven-year-old to attend their schools. The family also had all kinds of higher-end expenses, from the Peloton bike to meal subscriptions to new luxury cars. As a result, despite their relatively high income, they were drowning in credit card debt—more than $85,000 worth. It goes without saying that this is a situation you do not want to find yourself in. The problem here is a common one—and it was about spending, not income.

> Without a clear plan and a handle on your cash flow, no matter how much you make, the wheels can fall off.

This couple is not alone in allowing their spending to rise in proportion to their earnings. If you don't have a plan, and if you view every decision as transactional, then the more you make, the more you'll spend. Without a strategy, you're likely to make poor decisions. Without the success habits in place, you're susceptible to making very costly financial mistakes. I have known people who make over one million dollars a year and spend every dollar. They have nothing to show for their high earnings. When their business goes down, they're in big trouble, because they got used to the big lifestyle and didn't put anything away for their future.

As of this writing, the American economy is literally shut down because of the COVID-19 crisis. First-time jobless claims for the week ending 2/01/20 were 201,000, its lowest level since 11/15/69. Now, just three months later, according to the Department of Justice, over twenty-six million filed for jobless claims. What is most alarming is that prior to the shutdown, the record-breaking economy was going strong and personal wages were up. Despite that success, 59 percent of Americans surveyed in early February 2020 admitted they lived "paycheck-to-paycheck" and were not saving any money for emergencies or retirement.[8] I am a firm believer that even if you are living paycheck-to-paycheck, you can save *something*. When I first got married, I was making seven dollars an hour. We were young and broke. I always joke that I could vacuum our entire apartment and never unplug the cord because our place was so small! This is a philosophy grounded in my core—being resourceful, looking toward the future, and saving a portion of every paycheck you earn, no matter how small your paycheck is.

Unfortunately, the February 2020 study shows us that just before this unexpected global business disruption hit, the majority of

---

8   Schwab.com, "Schwab Modern Wealth Index Survey 2019," Schwab Brokerage, accessed April 16, 2020, https://www.aboutschwab.com/modernwealth2019.

people were *not* doing this. They weren't saving any money from their earnings. Now, those people are the ones who are most at risk financially. It's a dangerous place to put your family in.

The bottom line? Spending should not rise in proportion to a level of income, regardless of what that income is. You need the discipline to save and invest a portion of every paycheck, so that as your income rises, the percentage that you put away for your future will rise in proportion.

ASK THE RIGHT QUESTIONS

Instead of getting hung up on your investment return this year, ask yourself the important question: What is the monthly incoming cash flow I need to live comfortably? How much does my lifestyle actually cost? These questions apply whether you're working or in retirement, and its answer requires you to focus your planning around your spending and future sources of income.

> That personalized focus on something you can measure and adjust will impact your life in a way that an arbitrary percentage never can, because there's purpose attached. When it comes to your monthly cash flow, there is no right or wrong number—only *your* number.

For example, we've helped a wealthy, retired widow who felt embarrassed to tell us how much her spending had gone up. She said she was worried she might run out of money, and we braced ourselves for a super high number. It turned out, however, she was only spending $2,500 a month. I asked, "How are you even getting by here in Southern California? What are you doing? What are you eating?" We ended up having a funny conversation together. She realized in her mind she was spending a lot, but it was actually very little compared to the retirement portfolio they accumulated.

I've also designed an investment strategy to give a couple $150,000 of portfolio income per month to cover their expenses. They fall on the opposite side of the spectrum, with a lavish lifestyle, multiple beach houses, and a very large business generating significant income.

Everyone's situation is different, and your number is your number. There's no judgment attached to this step. The aim is to identify your goals, figure out how much they'll cost, and come up with a predictable lifetime income to keep you comfortable and allow you to live the life you want.

These contrasts illustrate there's no useful rule of thumb or magic number for your individual situation. One fact *is* universally true, though: once you have that reliable cash flow in place, the stress about money goes away.

DON'T MESS UP THE BACK NINE

When planning your income for your future, the two major factors individuals and financial advisors forget to account for are taxes and inflation. Ignore these at your peril! You'll regret underestimating their impact down the road. Sure, you can calculate your current income without help. This is where the rubber meets the road. When you've done that homework and taken the time to reflect on how your expenses might increase or decrease over time, you'll more than likely need to reach out to a professional to understand the impact of taxes and inflation.

Part of the exercise of using your current cash flow to project into the future involves considering what your sources of income will be when your paycheck stops. Specifically, you'll need sources of passive income in addition to whatever savings you've built up. If those income sources don't increase over time, they'll be eroded by inflation, which means you will be taking a lifestyle pay cut. In addition to your retirement investment accounts, do you have rental property? How much will your Social Security be? Do you have residual business income or annuities or insurance policies to draw from?

> Often, people don't match up all their future sources of income to their actual projected expenses. As a result, they keep putting away an arbitrary amount of savings and hoping it will be enough when they retire.

It's common for people to solely focus on the accumulation phase of life while ignoring the distribution phase of spending. That's like being a serious golfer and completely ignoring the back nine holes. Instead, we all know serious golfers pay attention: of those fourteen clubs in your bag, each have a purpose. You wouldn't dare step on to the course with only a putter or a driver. You may need your driver for the long par five on one hole, while your nine iron may work great off the tee box on a short par three. Sometimes, you'll find yourself hitting from a deep sand trap, and you'll need to pull out your sand wedge to make it onto the green. You have to be prepared for a variety of different situations on the course.

In reality, the important factor is not choosing a "retirement" age or some particular total dollar value in your accounts, but rather whether the income you have will cover what you need to spend over time—an income that is as diversified as the clubs in that skilled golfer's bag. That spending number doesn't have to be a mystery—you can and should come up with an accurate projection today.

DIVERSIFY AND DITCH YOUR STRESS

Until you get clear on your goals, determine your actual number, and build a plan from there, you're going to feel substantial stress and uncertainty. You won't be able to make big financial decisions without worrying if you can afford it. For instance, it's common for people in their later years to wonder if they should even be going on trips—even though travel was a key goal for their retirement. Until you have clarity, you won't have the means to kick out that anxiety.

There's an adage that says, "The best time to plant a tree was thirty years ago. The second-best time is today." It's best to diversify your sources of income in retirement so that you have a variety of trees, ones that bloom during different seasons and yield not only different fruits, but also shade for your family as part of your legacy. To accomplish this, you've got to begin planting different seeds as early as possible and nourishing the seeds you've already planted. You'd never want to rely on one tree to be the lone source of sustenance in your thirty-year retirement.

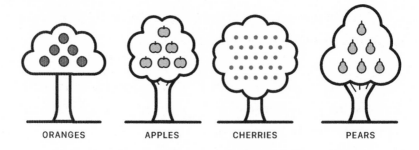

ORANGES   APPLES   CHERRIES   PEARS

Even though the best time to plant your tree was thirty years ago, it really *is* true that the next best time is today. You may avoid dealing with the details of your financial life because you think it's too late, or you might be afraid to face the facts and potentially realize the gap between where you could be and where you are. However, I encourage you to start the process without delay, because it's never too late to improve your circumstances and get on track.

KEY TAKEAWAYS

- Tracking your annual investment return and your total portfolio value is not as important as understanding your monthly cash flow.
- Visualize and verbalize what your ideal future lifestyle is like, and then estimate the cost of funding it as a monthly cash flow number.
- Determining your actual number sets the target you aim for. You should consider all the possible income sources that could fund that monthly number.

BIASED ADVICE FROM FINANCIAL SALESPEOPLE

"Don't be embarrassed to push, and if you don't get the answers you want, it's okay to walk away. If investors educate themselves and ask smart questions, they can ensure that they are getting quality, honest advice regardless of what happens with the law."

—JON STEIN, CEO OF BETTERMENT

What if I told you that about 95 percent of financial advisors don't have an obligation to put your interests first? Would that surprise you?

In a 2016 poll by the American Association of Individual Investors, 65 percent of respondents said that they didn't trust advisors, with just 2 percent saying they trust them "a lot" and 15 percent "a little." Why does such a large majority of the public distrust the financial advice industry? Perhaps it's because most people have encountered a high-pressure sales pitch from a broker, insurance agent, or other financial professional at some point in their life. Have you ever sat through a timeshare presentation in which the manager puts your feet to the fire about making the final purchase? How did that experience feel? I personally can't stand when someone is trying to pressure me into buying something, especially when I can tell the person cares more about closing the deal than they do about listening to my goals and helping me get what I need.

According to conventional wisdom, financial advisors are a nest of vipers. People generally place more trust and credibility in advice coming from a doctor, a lawyer, a CPA, or even an auto mechanic. Financial services has become the least-trusted industry in consumers' eyes after so many people have been taken advantage of or seen promises of investment success fall very short.

> It's no secret that Wall Street and the big banks prioritize profits and giving their shareholders an investment return, often at the expense of what's best for their clients.

Just look at the news. You can easily find financial scandals from financial advisors and institutions that have taken advantage of the very people who trusted them with their hard-earned money. Recently, Wells Fargo was in the news as one of the big banks to be fined and penalized for scandals that took advantage of clients. Here's just a quick timeline of the scandals in just the last few years:

- September 2016: Wells Fargo is fined $185 million for creating 1.5 million fake deposit accounts and over 500,000 fake credit cards for clients without their knowledge, so that employees could hit sales targets and the bank could charge them more fees.
- September 2016: It is also fined $20 million for repossessing cars from active-military duty members.
- March 2017: 1.4 million more fake accounts come to light.
- March 2017: Regulators find the bank isn't complying with community lending rules to serve lower-income populations.
- April 2017: A former Wells Fargo wealth manager turned whistleblower wins $5.4 million and reinstatement of his job.
- February 2018: Because of widespread compliance issues, the Federal Reserve restricts the bank's growth.

And that's just a partial list of what we know about, recently, from just *one* of the big banks!

THE PERILS OF BAD ADVICE

Suffering at the hands of big banks and bad advisors has real consequences for real people. Recently, a retired couple from San Clemente, California, came to our office for an initial consultation. They said their estate planning professional highly recommended us, and they were excited to find someone trustworthy to manage their finances. They are both retired and in their seventies, and they felt making investment decisions on their own provoked stress and anxiety. Their previous three financial advisors had generated the following outcomes:

- One lost 100 percent of an investment in what turned out to be a massive Ponzi scheme. In April 2019, the SEC charged the advisor with defrauding 8,400 investors (many of them senior citizens), ordered prison time, and demanded payback of over $1 billion.
- The second oversaw a decline of more than 20 percent in portfolio value in one quarter, despite promoting investments that would supposedly be appropriate for them as a retired couple and carry only "moderate risk."
- The third lost 100 percent of an investment in another Ponzi scheme.

It's no wonder this pair felt skittish about financial advisors. Can you blame them? I was surprised they even wanted to meet with us, considering how jaded their experience had surely made them. The sad part is the advisors who recommended those high-risk investments had big financial incentives to do so. They clearly were not looking out for their clients' best interest. After all of those significant losses, the couple had about $1.7 million left to provide for their entire retirement. While that amount is still enough to work with and provide for a comfortable retirement, they were over $500,000 short of what they'd had before—while living in one of the most expensive parts of the country (Southern California). Success would require some careful planning and decision-making—which we took on, starting (of course) with goals. They are now a few years in and feeling much more confident about their retirement. They won't be pitched any high-risk investment schemes from here on out.

In another case, we met with a wealthy couple in their late fifties who were not only seeking to work with an independent financial advisory team but looking for advice for the wife's parents as well. Because of the advanced age of her parents, the couple gave their previous brokers, advisors, and their staff firm instructions that all financial recommendations and transactions were to be approved by them first. As it turns out, the original advisor her parents worked with persuaded them to borrow millions against their portfolio to invest in distressed private businesses the advisor was personally affiliated with.

As if that weren't bad enough, one of the brokers at the firm pressured the parents to sell their high-value rental homes in Orange County, California, using his wife as the real estate agent. Furthermore, the "financial advisor" himself borrowed nearly $200,000 from them to help upgrade his vacation condo in Florida, promising a nice interest rate in return. (In case you were wondering, it's a very big no-no for a financial professional to borrow money from their clients.) The couple was furious after finding out about all these shenanigans and asked us to review their parents' (who were in their nineties) financial statements. It's sad stories like these about swindling trusting clients that give my industry a bad name.

THE BEAUTY OF FIDUCIARY DUTY

Fortunately, there's an alternative to the pushy financial sales-people. Not all financial advisors have such pressing conflicts of interest. Maybe you've heard the buzz over the past few years about the word "fiduciary." Fiduciaries are required to provide "the highest standard of care and trust" for their clients.

> A fiduciary professional must act in the beneficiary or client's best interest at all times. For a fiduciary financial advisor, this role may mean recommending a financial strategy that results in reduced or no compensation, simply because it's the best option for the clients.

According to the Securities and Exchange Commission, which regulates registered investment advisors as fiduciaries, the fiduciary duty also includes the following:[9]

- Acting with undivided loyalty and utmost good faith.
- Providing full and fair disclosure of all material facts, defined as those which "a reasonable investor would consider to be important."
- Not misleading clients.
- Avoiding conflicts of interest (such as when the advisor profits more if a client uses one investment instead of another or trades frequently) and disclosing any potential conflicts of interest.
- Not using a client's assets for the advisor's own benefit or the benefit of other clients.

---

9   "Commission Interpretation Regarding Standard of Conduct for Investment Advisers." Securities and Exchange Commission, n.d., https://www.sec.gov/rules/interp/2019/ia-5248.pdf.

With modern advancements in technology and transparency, it's shocking to me how most people still don't know if they work with a broker or a fiduciary advisor or why that distinction even matters. The vast majority of the more than 350,000 financial professionals in the industry are working as agents for their bank or insurance company, not as fiduciaries for their clients.

Advisor Model	Broker Model
Fiduciary	Suitability
Advice	Transactions
Transparency	Disclosure
Registered Investment Advisor	Investment or Financial Advisor
Third-Party Custody	In-House Custody
Ethics	Legality

WATCH YOUR BACK—BECAUSE THE BANKS AREN'T

I spent nearly nine years at a global investment bank in the private wealth management division. Managers held mandatory meetings with all staff multiple times a week. Behind the scenes, there was regularly some kind of "focus" for the firm that advisors were incentivized to sell to clients. The investment company offering higher commissions as well as more marketing money to the branch office would sponsor lunches and golf outings. Once the banks bought most of the investment firms (2008–2010), an increased focus on banking products and cross-selling initiatives spread like wildfire in the industry. Now, on top of the firm initiative to sell investment funds, there were cross-selling incentives to promote specific credit cards, mortgage loans, and even money market funds that paid higher internal fees to the bank.

We'd have staff meetings in which we were directed to move client cash into particular savings funds, which sounds harmless, except the result would be the client making less interest than before—a move good for the bank, but not for the customer. Clients would get calls and emails about such changes, but most wouldn't pay attention to the details. They assumed the banks would take good care of them. Those meetings and employee incentive programs always left a bad taste in my mouth. I was not popular with regional managers at that time, because I consistently resisted the pressure to just do whatever they were encouraging on behalf of the bank.

In the big banking industry, there's also so much paperwork filled with incomprehensible legalese that clients often have no idea what they're signing. Such documents are all about protecting the banks' interests rather than the clients.' Yes, banks and financial advice firms are businesses, and they have to make a profit. There's nothing inherently wrong with that. However, it's certainly possible to do so in a transparent, ethical, and client-friendly way. Unfortunately, most firms opt for being less clear and upfront rather than more so.

> The brokers at banks and insurance companies are, for the most part, very good people. They're not all a bunch of scam artists looking to swindle you out of your hard-earned money. However, the system and structure of their employment stacks the deck against you.

When advisors at big banks log in to their computers each morning, their main employee home page is all about the commissions and incentives they can earn by meeting particular sales quotas. That's their focus. The system inherently sets up a relationship of opposition rather than collaboration with the clients, because the advisors are incentivized to find as many ways as possible to charge their clients and please their bosses.

MY WAKEUP CALL

When I worked on that side of the industry back in 2004, one potential nonprofit client had an investment portfolio value well over $25 million. We were competing with a few other financial advisory groups to win the business and were fortunate and excited to be chosen by their committee after months of meetings and presentations. At the very end of the process, the vice chair of the nonprofit's board asked us to sign a form stating we'd serve as its financial fiduciary when managing the investments and always put their interests first. Uh oh. By nature of where we worked and our employment contracts, we were not fiduciaries.

I spoke with our regional management to see how we could get around this obstacle and what we could do, but unfortunately, there was no good answer. As a result, the nonprofit decided to rescind the decision and award the business to a different financial advisory team—a fiduciary one. It was devastating to me, but the experience taught me something important. Being an independent fiduciary matters. Clients who *do* know the difference are skeptical of financial advisors because they've been burned before and don't want to be taken advantage of for the sake of a commission or other undisclosed conflicts.

In the end, the increased pressure to do what was best for the bank instead of what was best for the client prompted me to leave the comforts of the big firm to start my own wealth management services business. I was completely done with the stuffy, corporate, bank-first environment and realized operating independently would offer the best future environment in an industry desperately seeking transparency. My mission would be to design financial strategies and offer personal advice based on the needs and priorities of clients, rather than the big corporation.

In making that big move from corporate investment advisor to independent fiduciary in 2011, I remembered the wise advice of my good friend's dad, a successful attorney and entrepreneur. When I was twenty-three years old and new to this industry, he said, "Just remember one thing: always take care of your clients first and foremost, and put them ahead of yourself. If you do this, your growth and success will take care of itself!" That advice never left me. By starting my own business in a fiduciary capacity, I could fully act on it.

IT'S ALL ABOUT THE PEOPLE

One of the things that attracted me to this industry in the first place is working directly with people. I wanted to be the trusted resource for families or business owners looking to achieve goals and needing some professional guidance to get there.

I learned so much during my almost nine years at Merrill Lynch. The challenge was big bureaucracy and constantly facing the conflicting priorities of the client and the big shareholder-owned bank. Like you, I saw the banking industry go through significant changes through the Great Recession of 2007 to 2009, many of which aimed to better protect the banks and the shareholder interest instead of making things easier, better, and more efficient for the clients who entrust us with their money.

For instance, banks devoted so much bureaucracy to protecting themselves and preventing lawsuits that personal communication was completely stifled. Advisors couldn't even go out to lunch with clients without completing paperwork and getting multiple layers of approval. You may not believe it, but we even had to get two separate people to sign an approval form before mailing out a birthday card. The regulations and restrictions put a real damper on personal service. The banks want their customers to be loyal to the institution, not the person they're communicating with about their financial life and personal goals. The result was completely taking the personal relationship out of the equation, even though helping people with their money involves addressing personal goals and concerns around finances.

You may recognize the quote, "No man can serve two masters." I felt caught in a tug-of-war between what was best for my employer (i.e., the big bank) pulling me on one side and what the clients were needing me to do on the other. I care about my clients as people—they're like family to me. Adding all kinds of barriers to connection and communication for the sake of protecting bank profits takes the human element out of personal advice.

The conflict I felt was eventually too much, so I had to choose. Either I would completely sell out and become a lifetime Wall Street corporate suit, or I'd have to take the jump, pull the rip-cord, and completely dedicate my career to focusing on clients. The latter would mean giving up all the corporate perks and industry traditions of being a big broker on Wall Street.

Leaving was a big deal. It meant kissing all the benefits goodbye, but I decided to go for it. I wanted to design a business 100 percent about the client experience. By having experts on my team and connections to outside top-notch professionals, I'd make sure I could field anything clients needed help with. Becoming an independent fiduciary was very important to me, because it separated my business from the majority of people out there giving financial advice.

> Transparency and trust are essential to success in your relationship with your financial advisor.

Now, we have the freedom to use the resources and the research from all the big companies without any pressure to sell their policies or products. That means I can sit across the table, confidently look someone in the eye, personally connect with them, and tell them why what we're suggesting is the right decision.

As you consider what's best for your financial future, be careful taking advice from any financial professional who is not willing to share both the pros and cons of the strategy they recommend.

BEEN THERE, DONE THAT

In personally connecting with my clients as a fiduciary, I also now understand what it's like to be a business owner and entrepreneur. Since many of our clients are entrepreneurs, they appreciate the fact that I've been in the trenches. I own multiple businesses now and can understand where they're coming from. By contrast, an employee of a Fortune 100 company advising an entrepreneur doesn't have direct experience being responsible for payroll and a lease, nor would they have firsthand understanding of the challenges of running a business during a recession.

It was both stressful and completely liberating to leave a big firm. I had to start over, but I also got to set my own rules. I had payroll, a lease, equipment, and all kinds of overhead without any clients initially. There was no guarantee anyone would come to work with me or hire me to be their advisor. However, it didn't take very long for us to gain the trust of existing and new clients and build a successful business. I felt so much more excitement to come to work every day from that point forward. You don't realize how much you're under the corporate thumb until you're gone. I can relate to people's breakaway and point-of-no-return stories about starting their own businesses.

In fact, we love working with first-generation entrepreneurs and wealth creators because we understand they're the backbone of the American economy. They take the leap of faith and believe they can solve a problem and make things better. They use their passion and innovation to create valuable businesses that we all benefit from. We consider them heroes and serve as the champions cheering them on. These clients have taken risks and made difficult personal choices, so we want to be there to help guide them to success.

> Fiduciaries succeed when you succeed. This describes what you deserve in a financial arrangement: the hero of the story is not the financial professional. The focus should remain on you and what matters to you and your family.

The more the fiduciary advisor listens and gives personalized advice rather than template or cookie-cutter input, the better the outcome. Trusted, experienced fiduciaries don't push a particular product of the day. Instead, they should elevate the story of each client.

NO ONE SHOULD WIN AT YOUR EXPENSE

I believe my job is to help clients win, and I make my living by helping them do so rather than looking to profit from confusing them or pressuring them into decisions. Brokers at big banks can win at the expense of their clients, whereas fiduciaries win together *with* their clients.

> There is potential upside and downside to everything you do with your money. A true fiduciary will give you the full story every time.

I don't believe financial advice should be free or even cheap, because it's a valuable service based on expertise. However, the cost should be aligned with the value provided. At big banks, every employee logs into their computer and sees data on commissions and quotas. It's right there on the screen all day, and that's not an accident. As a fiduciary, we log into our computers at work and see the names of each family we are working with, and the tasks we have as a team to help them, and the next steps in achieving their goals and priorities. It's a completely different perspective. We know that if we do right by our clients, they will be loyal and will be willing to introduce us to others who need advice and guidance.

We recently had a client who moved $2.5 million to our firm from a major bank. He loved his advisor there, which is somewhat rare, given the often-high turnover at big banks and the incentive to push high-fee products. However, even though he liked his advisor as a person, he said he couldn't be sure his advisor shared and prioritized his personal objectives.

The final straw came when his wife became very ill. They'd been paying on a long-term care policy for twenty-seven years and needed advice on how to use it in coordination with Social Security, Medicare, and so on. The bank restricted his advisor from giving that kind of advice, because such recommendations are beyond its profit scope and might risk getting sued for mistakes. It was then that the client realized it was time to move on, even though their professional relationship was solid. (I told the client that because his old advisor sounded like he was a good and caring person, I bet he'd probably become an independent fiduciary as well before long.)

My firm was able to offer more tailored services because we have a dedicated Medicare expert and a Social Security advisor. We could talk through the options with him and even get on the phone with his long-term care company to help him discover his options. We could talk through the questions the insurance company would ask him and walk through the entire process with him. There's no extra charge for him and his wife for the hour spent on that phone call. There's no conflict of interest in offering such help. He finds such coordinated service much more important than whether his investments made 9 percent or 8 percent last year. You need to work with an advisory team who makes your top priorities *their* top priorities.

DIFFERENT STANDARDS OF SERVICE

I want to make it clear that my point is not to bash Wall Street banks or seem like David yelling at Goliath. I've worked on both sides of the industry, so I can speak to both sides, including when it comes to the official standard of care.

A common situation for a Wall Street advisor would be to have two equally financially suitable funds available to a client, one paying a 1 percent commission and one paying a 5 percent commission. Obviously, the advisor has an incentive to recommend the latter investment fund over the former. A broker follows a suitability standard, which is a very low bar that essentially just says the investment choice could be justified.

Independent advisors following a fiduciary standard, on the other hand, have a much higher standard of care and service. They can't earn a commission at all; instead, they charge the client a flat fee or flat rate. As a result, there is no distortion in the recommendations, including to buy or sell more investment vehicles than needed. A fiduciary would simply recommend the least expensive fund offering the best investment opportunity.

> More than 90 percent of financial advisors operating today are brokers, not independent fiduciaries. If you're like most people, you probably had no idea about the difference. It's a safe bet that if you did, there'd be no contest between the two types.

WHAT YOU DESERVE FROM AN ADVISOR

When seeking financial guidance, you will benefit from independent and objective advice. Here are seven things to expect from an independent advisor:

① **They do not work for the same company where your financial account (or insurance policy) is held.** For example, if your money is at XYZ bank and your advisor also works at XYZ bank, that's a red flag if you want an independent fiduciary. Similarly, if you're buying a life insurance policy from ABC Insurance Company and your advisor works for ABC Insurance Company, that's also a red flag. Your options are limited when your broker or agent is "captive" and only offering investments and policies from their employer's menu.

② **They are fully transparent regarding the costs you will pay for investment management, financial planning, and investment trades made on your behalf.** Your independent fiduciary advisor will not work for commissions on investment trades and will likely charge a flat rate percentage for investment management. For financial planning, they will have either a one-time planning cost that is set in advance, an annual retainer, or an hourly planning fee.

③ **They will explain their process for selecting investments and create a written business plan for your money.** Do not give your money to any financial professional to invest without a clear and written strategy first. This will often be called an Investment Policy Statement. (Ours is called an Investment Strategy Guide®). You deserve to understand your advisor's process for researching and selecting investments for your money.

④ **They bring trust and integrity to the table.** Nothing is more important than these when it comes to finding and working with a financial advisor. You would be wise to speak with some references, do some research online, and find reviews they've been given. Look for how they answer your challenging questions. If you have to play detective, then it's time to move on.

⑤ **They have the right certifications and credentials.** Of course, your advisor should show proficiency and expertise through their education and experience. One caveat, though, is that I don't believe it's necessarily a good thing when someone has seven different credentials after their name. Sometimes, advisors spend more time reading books than actually serving clients and gaining the experience such real-world work entails. If you're seeking out retirement planning, for example, it's more important that your advisor be knowledgeable and experienced in retirement planning than how many credentials he or she has behind their name.

⑥ **They eat their own cooking.** In other words, they invest in the same kinds of financial vehicles they recommend, and they're successful and wealthy themselves. You probably wouldn't work with a personal trainer who's overweight and out of shape, because there's no evidence they know how to apply the principles they promote in their own life—or even that those principles work. The same goes for financial advisors.

⑦ **They have experience running a business (if that's important to your situation).** This won't apply to everyone, but if you're a business owner and an entrepreneur, I recommend working with an advisor who also has direct small business ownership experience. They'll understand in detail the considerations and challenges entailed—firsthand, not just in theory. Unless you have kids, you can't fully understand and appreciate what it's like to be a parent. Would you take parenting advice from someone with no kids? To me, the same goes for founding and running a business.

Finally, when you get referrals, do your due diligence. Make sure you conduct more research and do more independent vetting to justify handing over your hard-earned money than simply reviewing a website or hearing from a golf buddy about a particular advisor.

When assessing your financial advisor, ask questions like the following: Who makes money from my account, and how much?

What specific expertise do you have that applies to the goals I am aiming to achieve? Do you make more money recommending some investments over others? Are you committed to acting in my best interest for all my accounts, at all times?

> **KEY TAKEAWAYS**
>
> - Be very aware of incentives, conflicts of interest, and biases in the financial advice you receive—most professional advisors are brokers, not fiduciaries.
> - Vet and choose your advisor carefully. Don't be afraid to ask direct questions, and don't be afraid to walk away.
> - Work with a fiduciary who puts your best interests first, whose only priorities are to help you succeed, and who only wins when you win.

OBSTACLE 5

THE F-WORD

"When trillions of dollars are managed by Wall Streeters charging high fees, it will usually be the managers who reap outsized profits, not the clients."

—WARREN BUFFETT

A few years ago, a retired couple came to one of our offices to meet for the first time. They'd been an investment client of a large well-known financial institution and had no idea what they were paying in fees to be a client of the firm. While doing the initial analysis for them, we dug into their statements and learned they were paying 1.5 percent to their advisor plus another 1.4 percent of internal expenses, totaling almost 3 percent per year.

They were shocked.

"We're really paying *that much*? No one told us that," they'd said. "That's not what we expected. No wonder our investment returns have been so low. I can't believe that. She takes us to lunch a couple times a year, but other than that, she barely even calls us."

Their situation is shockingly common. Many people pay far too much and don't realize it until a third party comes along and assesses their situation in a comprehensive way.

When people learn how much they're paying in hidden fees, they understandably feel misled or taken advantage of. It causes a lot of distress. Unsuspecting investors fall prey to the wolves of Wall Street—the layers and layers of investment managers, middle managers, vice presidents, and regional vice presidents flying around in their private jets, taking brokers on special golf trips and going to Hawaii with all the commissions they make by hitting their quotas. Hidden fees line traditional brokers' and their managers' pockets, but financial advice doesn't have to work that way.

There *is* hope. In the internet age, it's relatively simple to determine what you're paying. Then, you can determine whether you're paying too much for too little value and make changes accordingly. Otherwise, you run the risk of excessively high fees in exchange for a limited scope of advice and services stunting your wealth's growth and affecting your long-term quality of life.

WALL STREET WANTS YOU CONFUSED

Something I've always despised about big banks and Wall Street is that they want information sharing with clients to be low. We are in the information age. When I first started at Merrill Lynch in 2003, it was uncommon for people to access stock and mutual fund quotes on their own—they'd instead call our office and ask the prices for specific companies. Trade orders took place over the phone, and we earned a minimum commission of 8.25 percent per trade. In other words, when someone invested $100,000 of their retirement account in Johnson & Johnson, I'd make $8,250 for a transaction that took me less than a minute to handle for them. Before market statistics and trading became easily accessible online, Wall Street loved having a monopoly on both information and pricing. The situation concentrated power in the hands of the brokers, whose clients depended on them for access.

Now, the internet has exploded the movement toward transparency. However, more information has *also* caused confusion; there's so much data available that people just throw their hands up. It's information-overload to the extreme. They feel like they can't figure out their finances on their own, and trying to navigate it all brings a lot of stress.

It's tempting to avoid stressful financial topics, but such avoidance comes with a cost. Knowing what you pay for financial advice is important. As NerdWallet's Kyle Ramsay said, "Everyone talks about the benefits of compounding interest, but few mention the danger of compounding fees." If you work with a skilled professional, you can conceivably only make the big financial decisions once and save substantial of money over time in the process.

NO FREE 401(K) LUNCH

More than a third of people think their 401(k) investments are free, and only 27 percent of Americans who participate in such a plan know how much they're paying in fees, according to a TD Ameritrade survey.[10] That's outrageous. Massive companies like Fidelity aren't charities; they're providing a real and valuable service. However, it's understandable that many investors are confused because the industry intentionally makes the fee structure complicated.

Of course, most investors aren't going to read the 200-page prospectus that comes along with a retirement investment account. They mistakenly assume all fees are inevitable and more or less the same across the different options. According to a recent report by Personal Capital, 61 percent of people don't know how much they pay in fees. About a third of people wrongly assume higher investment fees generally translate to higher returns.

If people *did* read each long prospectus, somewhere on page

---

10 "Ameritrade Investor Pulse Survey, January 2018." Ameritrade, n.d., https://s1.q4cdn.com/959385532/files/doc_downloads/research/FY2018/Investor-Sentiment-Infographic-401k-fees.pdf.

179 they might find out they paid 5 percent in upfront commissions that didn't show up on their monthly statement. They thought they invested $100,000, when really, they only invested $95,000—$5,000 off the top immediately went to the broker and the fund company. The client had no idea, because the fee wasn't clearly disclosed. These kinds of mistakes cost money that compounds over time and erodes your investment returns.

You may be wondering what, then, is a reasonable amount to pay in fees. It goes back to our magic number point: there's no hard-and-fast rule for what range of fees would be okay. In general, though, the more you can consolidate, the better deal you should get. Someone who invests $15 million will get a better rate than someone who invests $1 million. Regardless, there are many places where people pay fees but don't get value. The cheapest option isn't necessarily the best choice either. The important factor in making a good decision is transparency, so you can determine whether your costs are fair and appropriate for your circumstances.

When you work with a fiduciary, you'll see the costs and sign a form agreeing to pay those costs. No tricks, no gimmicks. The cost of services will clearly appear on your statement as a line item. On the other hand, if you're working with a broker instead of a fiduciary, you'll likely be paying commission and fees you cannot necessarily see because they're priced into the investment.

GETTING HELP AND PEACE OF MIND

To get the results you want, you need specialized, unbiased advice—and that advice is in short supply. For example, I personally don't know anything about cars. I honestly have no interest in learning about them, how they work, or the problems they have. Because of my lack of education in auto repair, I have no idea if what the mechanic tells me is true. One person could recommend a $6,000 repair telling me to replace the engine and the transmission, and another person could tell me I just need to get an oil change—I wouldn't know whether or not they were accurate or giving honest advice.

The biggest problem I see with this example of the auto mechanics is they get paid based on what they recommend I do. The fees they earn for the amount of repairs recommended create incentives that lead to a conflict of interest. It's a poor arrangement for me as a customer, because the more the mechanic recommends to repair or replace in my car, the higher the fee. I'm already inherently skeptical.

What if I could go to a third-party auto repair business who did a full diagnostic on my car for a flat fee and had no incentives or personal interest in making money from me based on what they find? I would really trust that person and their advice! No matter what they found, they'd make the same amount of money, so there'd be no reason for them to tell me anything other than the clear truth, spelling out what's working well in my car and what needs repair, along with the pros and cons of each recommendation.

Working with an independent, flat-fee fiduciary is like having access to that unbiased auto technician. In the case of the retired couple we discussed at the beginning of this chapter, their resolution and stress relief came from bringing clarity knowing and understanding what they were invested in and how much they were paying. We were able to reduce their total costs by 60 percent and shine a spotlight on what they pay for and why. They felt much better because they had transparency. They understood the value of independent advice and guidance and appreciated the upfront communication.

> Being in the dark about all the fees and commissions you're paying causes unnecessary anxiety. You should know how much you're spending and how your advisor makes money, in addition to setting up a comprehensive financial strategy that meets your goals.

If you pay for planning advice, there should be a clear, flat price tag on that advice—no hidden fees buried in an incomprehensible fifty-page agreement. Transparency and clarity will give you the confidence you need moving forward.

KEY TAKEAWAYS

- Unchecked and excessive fees will erode your returns.
- Advice and investment management services aren't free; however, make sure you are not overpaying and wasting money on high fees.
- Fiduciary advisors should charge a transparent, flat fee, and they shouldn't make more money unless they make you more money.

OBSTACLE 6

TAKING ON TOO MUCH RISK (OR NOT ENOUGH)

"Risk is incredibly important to investors. It's also...very hard to recognize, especially when emotions are running high. But recognize it we must."

—HOWARD MARKS, CO-FOUNDER OF OAKTREE CAPITAL

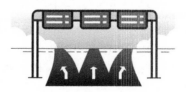

Consider this scenario, a true story that I witnessed during my early years at the big brokerage firm. A woman walks away from a divorce with $2.5 million, thinking she is getting the better deal. (Her ex-husband takes home $2 million in the form of their house and the 401(k).) Her $2.5 million investment account is primarily invested in one tech company stock (WorldCom) and seems to be going up in value each month. This woman's money, however, did not last. She was enamored with tech stocks and was caught up in the hype. Her advisor tried many times to warn her about the risks of being too concentrated in one stock position. To her, at the time, that allocation didn't seem *that* risky, because she was making so much money at first. If you can think back to 2000–2002, many investors had those same blinders on with regards to tech stocks, just like the irrational exuberance in 2005–2007 with real estate investors. However, after the tech bubble burst and the decline in her account kept accelerating, she refused to believe it was really happening. She hung onto the stock until WorldCom filed for bankruptcy in July of 2002. Her money was literally all gone. What was the woman's mistake in this situation? To start, clearly, she'd taken on way too much risk.

At the other extreme, people often mistakenly assume that risk means there is a chance an investment could go down in value. According to financial guru, Nick Murray, the greatest risk you actually face is your money losing its purchasing power. If you stash your money under a mattress and lose ground to inflation, you will see how in the future your money might buy half as much as it used to, or more. Inflation is the silent wealth killer.

We've seen many stories from both ends of the spectrum— people taking on way too much risk and gambling their family's future as well as people sitting on the sidelines with idle and dusty money, watching the value of it slowly erode.

> The right way to approach risk—and the way that will take the most stress off your plate—is to find a middle path that suits your goals, age, and retirement plans.

As you might have guessed at this point in this book, your clear, written, goals-based financial plan will determine the exact approach that makes sense for you.

THE RIGHT AMOUNT OF RISK

Finding the "just right" amount of risk is part of solving Obstacle 1. When you have a goal and a plan to achieve it, you can work backwards and calculate an appropriate level of risk for your investments. When you have no plan and no clear goals, when you're consuming the financial fast food every day, and when you're following biased advice from financial salespeople, your risk will end up out of whack with your circumstances because you'll have no frame of reference.

THE THREE-BUCKET STRATEGY

Some people approach risk and diversification by using a strategy with three "buckets." The first is money you'll potentially need in the next two years, which you can access in a safe savings account tomorrow if you need it. When you have an appropriately stocked first bucket, you get peace of mind from knowing you have the money you need to cover expenses that pop up—even if the markets tank after political elections, you lose your job, or a major emergency comes up. Other people who don't have clearly defined goals and adequate savings are likely to get spooked by news of market swings or trade wars. They may make bad decisions regarding this and other buckets locking in permanent losses that will negatively affect their standard of living down the road.

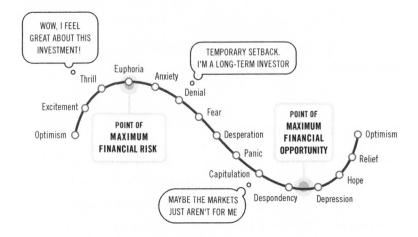

The second bucket earns more interest income than a savings account but is still relatively safe. The investments in this bucket aren't as much growth-focused as they are income-focused. They are typically not as available as money in your savings accounts, but they shouldn't necessarily be unreachable either. This bucket should give you a diversified cash flow from your portfolio and help balance the overall values during temporary stock market declines.

The third bucket is for long-term aspirations and goals, such as saving for retirement, with a time horizon of at least ten years. This bucket includes stocks, real estate investments, and other growth-focused strategies—the value goes up and down often, with an eye to higher growth over time through accepting higher risk.

When thinking about risk, it's important to appropriately fund all three buckets without overloading any of them at the expense of the other.

Remember, your investment portfolio is the servant of your financial plan and personal goals. You need sufficient funds available at all times in case your family has a medical emergency, the income earner in your family is temporarily out of work, or some other unexpected expense arises when the markets are down. For example, right now (March 2020) as COVID-19 has literally shut down most of the economy, people who need to access money to pay their bills should be dipping into their first "bucket." (Note: however, you also wouldn't want to overload your first bucket, or your money won't even keep up with inflation.)

I know what you're wondering, and the answer is no. Just like there's no magic number in your savings account you need to hit to retire, there's no magic formula for what proportion of risk belongs in each bucket. It doesn't make sense for everyone to divide their money into even thirds regarding risk. The right mix depends on your specific goals, age, and situation. If you are seventy-five years old and retired, for example, your needs are much different than your granddaughter who may have just graduated from medical school and is at the front-end of her earning years.

WHY ARE YOU EVEN INVESTING?

The only two real reasons to invest are to:

- Generate cash flow today
- Generate cash flow in the future

Determining the appropriate level of risk for your financial plan comes from first deciding which of those two lines up with your goals. Let's look at a couple of examples to illustrate this point.

A bucket allocation strategy for a forty-five-year-old high-income business owner should not be designed for current income. She doesn't need to rely on her investment portfolio to pay for her lifestyle yet. She may have 70 percent of her funds in the growth bucket, 25 percent of her funds allocated to her income bucket, and 5 percent allocated toward her safety and reserves bucket. Because of her high income, her cash flow will replenish every month. If you are in a similar phase, you don't need a large chunk of your money sitting idly in a savings account, because you have significant new money coming all the time. In that case, the money you earned last month should be put to work quicker, and productively invested for you with a goal of long-term growth.

A seventy-five year-old retiree, by contrast, may have a nearly opposite allocation, with 30 percent in the growth bucket, 55 percent in the income bucket, and 15 percent in the safety bucket. This fits better because their primary goal is monthly cash flow today, and they're looking for more income now rather than long-term growth for income at some future date.

Here's the bottom line: your age, goals, and situation determine what you prioritize. Too often, people want financial advisors simply to double their money or hit another arbitrary number.

Why? Are you planning to use it now or later, and how much do you or will you need? Those are the questions that must be answered before you invest. Remember the progression and foundation: goals → plan → investment strategy.

GOALS ⟶ PLAN ⟶ INVESTMENT STRATEGY

GOLDILOCKS YOUR PORTFOLIO

It's rare for a new client to come to us with a well-defined plan and a portfolio that aligns with that plan, even though they've usually worked with financial advisors previously. Unfortunately, they've often been pitched a few ideas and don't have any idea how all of it fits together.

As a result, it's very common for you to end up with a collection of investments that don't go well together and don't align well with your goals and risk comfort level. If you're like many people, maybe you tend to have either far too much in savings or not nearly enough; rarely do we see incoming clients who have a good balance appropriate to their situation.

Sometimes a client—say, a retired couple with a nice pension—will tell us they're risk-averse and don't want to lose money. When we actually look at their account statements, though, we'll find that they've invested aggressively like a pair of twenty-five-year-old gamblers and have lost 20 percent in the past year. The odds are that they had no idea because they had no clear plan in place. They were also likely working with an investment broker or salesperson instead of a professional fiduciary.

Other times, a younger client—say, a wealthy small business owner under forty—will think he's taking too much risk, but when we examine his financial life, it's just the opposite. He needs to be investing for growth instead of sitting on dusty money or overfunding his savings accounts like an eighty-five-year-old retiree. The business owner may simply be paralyzed by not knowing what to do with his money or whom to trust. So he decides to do nothing because it feels safe and prudent. As a result, he's missing out on potential growth and potential tax benefits. What we find all too often is that people aren't mentally accounting for the compounding effect of inflation. Look, for example, at the long-term historic inflation rate of 3 percent. Put simply, that means it will cost upwards of $2.40 in your thirtieth year of retirement to buy what a dollar buys today. If your income is substantially fixed-in bonds, CDs, and things of that nature, rising living costs may overwhelm it at some point.

> We all unconsciously default to the assumption that the essential financial issue in retirement is locking down our principal somehow. But it isn't. The essential issue is to create an income that rises ahead of inflation.

NO SUCH THING AS "NO RISK"

Some risks are inevitable, and some are unnecessary. Inflation risk is one of the inevitable ones. There's going to be inflation over time, and you'll have to deal with it. Market risk is another inevitable one; if you invest in the markets, there will be volatility. They'll go up and down in cycles. You can't completely avoid volatility if you're looking for growth. It's a simple fact that investing will be volatile.

> Let's make an important distinction here: volatility is not the same thing as risk. You've got to make that choice: on which end of your investing lifetime do you want your insecurity, so that you can have security on the other end?

You can certainly have blissful emotional and financial security on *this* end of your remaining lifetime—right here, right now. You could get a money market fund, a six-month CD at the bank, and some short-term Treasury bills. The dollar value of your account will barely fluctuate at all. You'll get a little bit of current interest each year, which will be more than wiped out by inflation and taxes, but you'll sleep like a baby. Of course, one day—and that day may not come for twenty years—you'll run out of money.

It's like exercising. You can go through the discomfort and potential pain of exercising now and reap health into your later years, or you can skip exercising now and be more likely to experience that pain and loss of health in your later years. In exercise and finances, it comes down to the same choice: pain now and comfort later, or comfort now and pain later?

Either way, one fact remains: you cannot control risk. However, you can manage and control how you respond to it, how you prepare for it, and how much risk you decide to take on. I have friends who invest in private businesses and real estate deals where they could lose 100 percent of their money, but they get an almost addictive thrill from making those high-risk gambles. Most of the time, it doesn't end well. The vast majority of people do not have enough surplus wealth to make getting involved in such investments a reasonable idea.

I once had a client who brought in a large sum of money for us to invest for his family—over 10 million dollars. Against our advice, he got excited and sucked into nearly every potential private deal that came across his desk—flipping houses for $2 million here, buying a shopping center for $3 million there, speculating with oil-digging projects in other states. He continually sold investments we made for him to fund these ideas. None of these high-risk endeavors paid off, and he's not a client anymore. He no longer has the money to invest.

In my experience, the successful investor is someone who remains receptive to sound, tailored, well-researched advice and uses it to pursue their goals. One of the most valuable skills for a professional fiduciary or financial planner to exercise is persuading people to make good decisions (and stick to those decisions) in times of high stress and uncertainty—that is, quite literally, my job. I'm here to guide people to do what's right for them even when their feelings try to compel them to do otherwise. Many people succumb to their emotions and make poor financial decisions. Even though they've shown patterns of being disciplined in the past, they suddenly hear something that sounds too good to be true, and they can put their entire family's financial life at risk. Unfortunately, I've seen this happen.

Here's a perfect example: as I am editing this section of my book (on February 27, 2020), the stock market had its largest point drop *in history*—1,190.95 on the Dow Jones Industrial Average. The news media is extremely hyped about the potential pandemic called the coronavirus. The well-known stock market indexes are down 12 to 14 percent in just the past week. People are panicking, and the headlines are sounding alarms. It's so tempting for you to get caught up in your feelings and abandon your plan in situations like this—which is one of the biggest risks you will face.

IPO FAILS

A client who was in the habit of consuming financial fast food media once got excited about a particular company's initial public offering (IPO). He wanted us to invest $50,000 of his retirement account in this stock that was soon to be available to the public. We told him the investment wasn't in line with his goals, but because the amount represented less than 2 percent of his account, we could make the small investment for him without it derailing his overall plan if it didn't go well. However, as he continued listening to various enthusiastic financial journalists and friends who were caught up in the hype, he decided he actually wanted to invest $500,000 rather than $50,000. That meant he'd be risking 20 percent of his retirement on a newer, unproven company.

My team and I tried to talk to him and his wife about the request. We tried everything in our power to help them see the risk far outweighed the potential return. Though potential growth feels exciting, the risk of losing money is extremely dangerous at that level. How much time did it take them to accumulate that $500,000? In retirement, you're taking income out of your IRA every month to live on and pay your bills. If you buy $500,000 worth of a single new company and it doesn't perform, your daily lifestyle takes a hit because you risked so much on one idea. Did they really want to take that chance?

After a full week of many conversations, emails, and phone calls, we successfully convinced the couple the investment was not in line with their goals. He was a bit frustrated and upset, but his wife felt very relieved that he wasn't going to take the big gamble. He had real FOMO and felt like he was losing out because all his friends were making big investments in the IPO. He couldn't believe we weren't on board when "everyone" knew it would go up in value. It was an "obvious winner." However, within the first two weeks, the stock was down 63 percent. He would've lost more than half of his investment in less than a month, when the money had taken more than a decade to accumulate. Imagine how they would've felt. Suddenly, he didn't feel left out as his friends either moaned with regret or made excuses for why the stock flopped out of the gate.

> Often, I look at an IPO like the "bad boyfriend." Everyone in the family can see the sister is dating a guy who is bad news, except for her. She thinks he's perfect and exciting, and she can't understand why her family isn't more welcoming of him. Then, when the relationship goes south, she wonders why no one warned her about him sooner.

As a financial advisor and professional fiduciary, I'm on the outside of the relationship looking in with objectivity and awareness of the larger plan. I don't lose my head to the next big trend the way the sister loses her head to love the bad boyfriend.

When we evaluate investment opportunities, we look at the facts, the costs, and what the outcomes will be if the investment goes well or poorly—will the risk justify those potential outcomes? Having a neutral fiduciary advisor can help prevent you from getting overly enthusiastic about a bad investment just because it seems appealing and exciting in the moment.

If you feel caught up in an IPO craze, it's important to ask yourself how much a bad outcome would impact your family and your goals. Usually, it's drastic. Of course, sometimes IPOs go well, too. If our client hadn't invested in that particular company and it had *gained* 63 percent instead of dropping that much, he surely would have been upset with us. However, such regrets represent hindsight bias. It's tempting to look at an outcome and believe that before it happened, you could feel what was coming or accurately predict the future.

Naturally, everyone likes to take credit when their investments go up and blame someone else when they go down. This psychology presents the core challenge of my field—we have to exercise logic in the face of impulsive human nature and strong emotions to achieve positive financial outcomes. A great fiduciary advisor needs to not only insulate you from short-term investment volatility, but also minimize your long-term regret and keep you from making big mistakes. When there's a lot of money at stake, people tend to lose their cool. When IPOs are successful, they stir up envy and regret in investors who didn't get in on the ground floor. However, those same investors would despair if they lost a chunk of their retirement funds they worked decades to accumulate. Why would you stake your future quality of life on a single company? Is it worth it?

ASSESS YOUR RISK

When considering your own comprehensive financial plan, make sure you've thoroughly assessed your risk. You need to know what's appropriate for your situation and that your investment allocation matches accordingly. You should be evaluating risks beyond your investments. These include risks of job loss, the primary family income earner passing away, extended healthcare expenses, home loss, or a significant decline in your business—to name a few. Your fiduciary advisor should go through a comprehensive diagnostic that examines every area of your financial life and risk exposure, including the following:

- Retirement planning scenarios
- Cash flow planning
- Taxes
- Social security benefits
- Pension analysis
- Disability insurance
- Long-term care insurance
- Life insurance
- and more.

This analysis will turn up gaps and ask questions that you and your family likely never considered. For the best results, review your financial inspection with an objective, neutral, third-party fiduciary whose team has expertise in these different financial planning areas.

KEY TAKEAWAYS

- Some risk is evitable, but a lot is unnecessary—and not even recognized by investors.
- It's incredibly hard to know what risks you're exposed to when you have a fragmented financial life.
- Protect your hard-earned success by knowing what risk level is appropriate for you to take on, which you can determine by creating a detailed, written, goals-based financial plan.

OBSTACLE 7

LETTING FEELINGS GET IN THE WAY

"The reality is that 99 percent of the time, the right thing to do is stick with the plan you've laid out and not react to short-term events. There are mountains of research showing the average investor return lags far behind the return of the overall market, and the reason for this gap is investor behavior."

—RYAN FRAILICH, FOUNDER OF DELIBERATE FINANCES

You may be wondering why, in a financial book, I've devoted a whole chapter to feelings. The answer is simple: in the real world of financial planning, the greatest analysis-based financial strategies and perfect plans can fall apart in five minutes if you let your feelings take over. There are many good places for your feelings. When it comes to money, though, unless you're talking about being charitable, they have no place.

I've seen even very smart people completely abandon their long-term plan at a moment's notice. Far too often, people's feelings lead them to abort their mission and jump ship. As I mentioned earlier, this week of editing the book (February 28, 2020) is a week of high emotions and panic. The news around the coronavirus pandemic threatens the entire world, and the stock markets just had their worst week of decline since the 2008 real estate bubble popped. We are now three weeks into March, and the financial markets are down 35 percent to 39 percent in just one month. It may seem like it's time to get out—but that's exactly the opposite of what you should do. That's why, in the realm of finance, it's essential to learn to manage your emotions and make decisions logically.

> As you get in the habit of maintaining perspective and referring back to your personal financial plan, you'll become less easily influenced by impulses that pop up in the moment.

WHAT YOU SHOULD DO VERSUS WHAT YOU FEEL

In finance, the two emotions you need to learn to recognize and temper are fear and greed. In essence, everything comes down to those two impulses. People make decisions based on overconfidence and irrational excitement about easy growth—or based on extreme fear of losing money. The latter group includes anyone like my grandparents, who lived through the Great Depression and saw banks fail. They didn't have any trust in the system, and they taught their children, my parents' generation, that banks could disappear and take their money. People are genuinely fearful of what they don't understand.

> "Investing is the age-old never-ending emotional battle between fear of the future and faith in the future."
>
> —NICK MURRAY

Wherever you tend to fall on the emotional spectrum, investing often feels like a roller coaster, with high highs and low lows. One day you're greedy, excited, and exuberant; the next, you're worried, and concerned, and the world seems to be ending. Then, you're desperate and despondent, wanting to throw in the towel. The problem is, your emotions aren't a good guide. In the world of finance, what you should do and what you *feel* you should do tend to move in opposite directions.

When stocks are extremely cheap and everything's on sale (like this week), instead of feeling sad and concerned, you should actually be aggressively buying. The stock market rises about four out of every five years, or about 80 percent of the time. Said another way, the market only falls 20 percent of the time. You can fear that 20 percent or cheer for it. The market dips are when you should be doing the opposite of the crowd. Yes, there *is* a place for intuition in investing, but it has to have the support of data and analysis. Without analysis, everyone would just validate what they felt. You can distinguish yourself by marrying instinct with strategy. In fact, today, we took action in our clients' portfolios by doing the opposite of what everyone's feelings would suggest. We sold a good portion of our bond investments and bought into our stock investments, since the stock markets are down 12 percent to 15 percent (depending on which index you look at).

It's also important not to let sentimentality cloud financial decisions. For instance, people sometimes inherit a spouse's or parent's company stock. They feel emotionally attached to the company, saying, "I can't sell any of this because it was my husband's or my dad's, and he worked there for his whole career," or "My wife bought this stock before she passed away, and it reminds me of her." These are delicate issues, but when your investments have sentimental value, it's a problem. Letting emotions enter into the financial planning process is bound to result in big mistakes, because you're following feelings over facts. You can have your own feelings, but not your own facts. When you're analyzing options and making financial decisions, your emotions should not take precedence over data.

Feelings can go either way, causing you either to take too much risk or sit on the bench without ever getting into the game. For example, I know a couple with a wife who grew up in a family without much financial education. Money was scarce and caused a lot of worry. Her parents reinforced risk aversion through the frequent refrain of, "We can't afford that—we're going to run out of money." Now, the couple has means, and their business is financially successful. But she's still paralyzed by the fear of running out of money. As a result, she doesn't enjoy the abundance they have. She hoards everything in her savings account, because it feels safe. Her husband wants to replace their twenty-year-old carpet and couches, and she adamantly refuses, saying they cannot afford it. If they invested the funds sitting in their savings account, though, they'd earn enough interest in two weeks to pay for the upgrades. But she's so fearful of running out of money that she lets it sit there without investing it. In her mind, everything is fine as long as nobody ever touches the account.

As this woman's situation illustrates, unchecked fear leads to bad outcomes because of missed opportunities. On the flip side, unchecked greed leads to excessive risk and potentially losing everything. People who let greed take over get blinded to the potential downsides of their actions. They think whatever they touch will turn to gold, and they aren't satisfied with the return they have—they want to triple it just because they think more is better.

> You can opt to enjoy life and remove your stress about money by choosing a third path, one characterized by strategy, integration, and planning, so you don't get knocked off course by either emotional extreme.

FACING YOUR FEAR

A surprising 61 percent of Americans say they are more scared of running out of money than they are of dying. Among those aged 44–49, that number climbed to 77 percent. And a whopping 82 percent of those in their late forties who are married with children feel that way, too.[11] On some level, we can probably

---

11 "Reclaiming The Future." Allianz Life Insurance Company of North America, n.d., https://www.allianzlife.com/-/media/files/allianz/documents/ent_991_n.pdf.

all relate to the worry we won't have enough to last until the end of our lifetime once we stop working. People don't want to live in poverty or become a burden on their children. Part of your fiduciary advisor's main role in helping you manage your financial life is eliminating your fear of running out of money.

One common fear response we see is people electing to take their Social Security income prematurely because they're so fearful the Social Security program will disappear by the time they reach their full retirement age.

WHEN PEOPLE CLAIM SOCIAL SECURITY

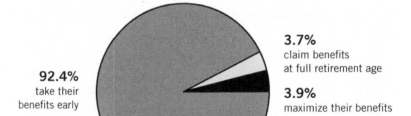

92.4%
take their
benefits early

3.7%
claim benefits
at full retirement age

3.9%
maximize their benefits
by waiting to age 70

Ninety-two percent of Social Security recipients take their benefits before reaching full retirement age. That compares to just under 8 percent waiting beyond full retirement age.[12]

---

12 Caplinger, Dan. "What's the Most Popular Age to Take Social Security? A Foolish Take." *USA Today.* Gannett Satellite Information Network, June 19, 2018, https://www.usatoday.com/story/money/ personalfinance/retirement/2018/06/19/whats-most-popular-age-to-take-social-security/35928543/.

> When you claim your income benefit prematurely, at age sixty-two, you are accepting between a 30 and 45 percent permanent pay cut for the rest of your life.

It's absolutely a fear response to say, "Well, I don't care if I'm going to get a 45 percent permanent pay cut from what the government actually owes me after I've paid in all these years." It's an irrational decision indicating a lack of planning. Plus, it's a permanent decision; once you turn that faucet on, you can't go back. It affects your monthly cash flow for the rest of your life. Often such people simply heard from a neighbor or friend that the program was going to go away and they'd better get their checks while they can. The situation is extremely common.

People also fear investing in general, because it comes with a degree of uncertainty. The average investor lacks technical knowledge around finance and markets. What if you come up with a good plan but don't stick to it? What if you make a mistake and your children aren't taken care of? What if you invest in the wrong place or your income dries up? These are questions a comprehensive financial plan can and should address, so you won't have to keep looping on worries.

> It's difficult for people to distinguish between genuine market risk and mere volatility.

It's human nature to fear what we don't know. Financial markets are complex, and we are overloaded with alerts and information. Our instincts signal us to retreat or keep us stuck doing nothing, because we feel overwhelmed and don't understand. Most of us would rather not even think about the financial future and just bury our head in the sand. Plus, some people are afraid of what they might learn if they really dig into their past financial mistakes and see the missed opportunities clearly.

Avoiding going to a financial advisor is a lot like avoiding the doctor. Maybe you don't go to a doctor because you haven't been eating well or exercising, and you're pretty sure your cholesterol is too high. It might be embarrassing or stressful to confront the truth, especially if you know confronting it would mean you'd need to make changes. Similarly, it's common for people to keep putting off addressing their finances, figuring they can deal with the issues later. They hope by the time they're in their sixties, everything will just work out. Human nature leads us to avoid pain, and sometimes the truth feels painful enough to keep us from taking action. However, you can't set yourself up for the future through avoidance.

Furthermore, fear and avoidance affect more than just you—they affect the people you love. Family members who depend on you will also gain or lose depending on how well you plan. As in the Social Security example, the permanence of many financial decisions is serious. When you make decisions based on your amygdala firing off fight-or-flight impulses, you probably won't like the results.

If the markets are down substantially and you take your $1.5 million retirement money that's not being taxed today, cash out the whole account to put it in your bank, and pay $600,000 in taxes, you've made a permanent decision with big consequences. If you don't have someone you trust and rely on to stand between you and your emotions, you're bound to make such mistakes, and they'll cost you. These are extremely expensive mistakes but also extremely common ones, because left to our own devices, most of us go with our feelings instead of a plan. It's human nature.

> All the failed investors I've ever encountered up close were continually emotionally reacting to current events—and always the wrong way.

In contrast, working with a qualified fiduciary, you can develop more financial responsibility by having them serve as a neutral third party with your best interests in mind. While your financial responsibility and confidence in your goal-focused strategy grows, your stress will shrink.

YOU DON'T HAVE CONTROL

Failing to demonstrate financial responsibility in the face of worry leads to big mistakes. I met a man at a charity fundraiser who lamented his big decision to cash out his portfolio a few years ago. He was so worried about the potential impact of the 2016 election, which he thought might bring some kind of financial Armageddon, that he cashed out his $4 million portfolio the day before. As it turned out, the markets did not crash—and he missed out on about $900,000 of growth over the previous three years by sitting on the sidelines with his money in a savings account at the bank. His irrational behavior was based on fear and perceived control rather than a realistic plan.

> Converting all your investments to cash at once in response to fear will not work out the way you want it to, because you have to time the market perfectly getting out *and* getting back in.

When people think they'll just wait out a potential downturn and then get back in the market, they tend to lose out. A major challenge for investment timing is most growth happens in a very short window. Of the 252 days a year the financial markets are open, 85 percent of the annual growth comes on just six of those days. Most people don't realize if they act on emotions and miss those best six days but are invested the other 246 days, the results will be almost like they weren't there at all. Growth is not a straight line or a steady climb. Portfolios go up and down and then have bursts of growth. Two of the best days in the stock market just happened in the past three weeks (March 2020), during the high volatility and the peak fear of the COVID-19 global pandemic. That reinforces my point: you cannot predict when the markets will bounce up. When you make emotional decisions out of fear and jump out, it's likely you'll miss the entire year's growth. You might be a little scared when the roller coaster goes upside down, but it's a better long-term strategy to stay on the coaster than to jump off the ride while it's moving.

> Long-term success doesn't come from *timing* the markets, it comes from time *in* the markets.

Fear-based decisions come from the perceived ability to exert control, when in truth, you have to work with financial reality. You can't eliminate all risk, and trying to do so will only subject you to loss by inflation. Perceived control also leads people to take greater risks than they realize. Maybe your business relates to shipping, so you put your entire investment portfolio into UPS and FedEx stock. Knowing the shipping industry well as a result of your personal career makes you feel you somehow have a little bit of extra control and knowledge. However, that overconcentration makes your entire cash flow (both your paycheck from work and your investment portfolio) dependent on a single industry.

Similarly, a lifelong realtor might only personally invest in real estate. They "feel comfortable" because they're investing in the one industry they have already learned about. They have some rental properties and nothing else, because they know real estate and feel like they have more control over it. Their fear of what they don't know causes them to put all their eggs in one basket. They don't trust guidance from someone who knows what they don't know, and they take on more risk rather than less as a result.

GETTING A GRIP ON YOUR GREED

A woman in her sixties, who was a friend's client, worked as a school principal and was a couple years away from retirement. I never met her, but I will never forget hearing the advisor tell me this sad story. Besides being a school principal, she also had a small family business on the side. Between the funds she and her husband had saved as well as forty years of growth, she'd built up a substantial retirement account. In the hysteria of bitcoin in December 2017, she elected to fire her financial advisors. She and her husband sold out of all the investments in their entire IRAs, worth about $1.5 million, and paid $600,000 in income taxes by cashing out. They put the remaining $900,000 all in bitcoin.

The original idea came from her high school grandson, who was extremely hyped up about the cryptocurrency and thought it would go over $100,000. She bought in when coins were valued at $17,900, and the investment very quickly dropped 60 percent. She turned $1.5 million into less than $450,000 (after income taxes and then the depreciation in bitcoin) in under two weeks. Her tragic experience demonstrates what making emotional investment decisions in the realm of greed can do to your financial situation in a shockingly short amount of time. Eighteen months away from retirement, when they'd saved for forty years, this couple drastically changed their retirement prospects by losing two-thirds of their savings…and completely unnecessarily.

During this same time period at the end of 2017, I got tons of calls and inquiries about bitcoin from people seeking recommendations, including my own extended family members. They were shocked to learn we'd invested zero client dollars in cryptocurrency, and that we were not recommending such speculative gambling to anyone. We don't indulge in the financial fast food news media and the hype, and we certainly didn't feel that the speculation risk was a good fit into our client's goal-based investment strategies.

Similarly, around 2007, I remember buying groceries at our local Stater Bros. and listening to a conversation between the cashier and grocery bagger about going to an auction to buy real estate to fix up and flip. I honestly couldn't believe it. New TV shows were popping up every week about how easy it was to get rich by borrowing money to buy properties and flip them with just a few weeks of work. A bell rang in my head that this conversation was yet another red flag, because minimum-wage employees at the grocery store were talking about how easy it was to make big bucks flipping properties. It didn't make sense. Soon thereafter, the Great Recession of 2007 to 2009 hit, and real estate lost more than 50 percent of its value.

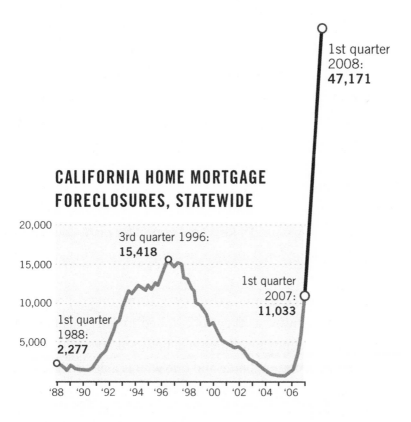

1st quarter 2008: **47,171**

CALIFORNIA HOME MORTGAGE FORECLOSURES, STATEWIDE

3rd quarter 1996: **15,418**

1st quarter 2007: **11,033**

1st quarter 1988: **2,277**

20,000
15,000
10,000
5,000

'88 '90 '92 '94 '96 '98 '00 '02 '04 '06

Those are the kinds of warning signs most people either don't see or completely ignore. They get caught up in the emotion and want to make sure they don't miss out on the next big payday. I get it. It's human nature for you to get excited about any chance to make money quickly. However, such seemingly get-rich-quick opportunities typically do not represent reality. People make the biggest mistakes exactly when they're the most hyped up. Remember this rule of thumb: if something seems too good to be true, it probably is.

ADVISORS ARE HUMAN, TOO

Unfortunately, the majority of financial professionals are susceptible to the same emotional mistakes regular investors make. In fact, in 2008, I remember many financial advisors at Merrill Lynch were overcome by the declines and paralyzed by fear, feeling the same emotions their clients were going through. Being under ten years in the industry at that time, I felt disappointed and almost embarrassed of our industry when I saw these experienced "financial professionals" falling apart and emotionally cowering after being in the business twenty to thirty-five years (that they spent preaching about the importance of sticking to your plan and maintaining composure). I lost some respect for many colleagues as I saw them abandon their own discipline and give in to the fear.

In the midst of economic crisis, everything they'd preached went out the window as they succumbed to worry. There is a tremendously important difference between an advisor who falls into that emotional hole and one who is able to serve as a steady guide and a coach with a crystal-clear process. It's not that good advisors don't feel emotions or that they only understand facts and logic. Rather, we have a well-defined process to follow in any particular economic and market circumstance with our clients—and there's a reason for that. As a client, you should absolutely have an agreed-upon process and guidelines with your advisor.

Your advisor should have demonstrated success during past times of high stress and volatility. When interviewing financial advisors, ask permission to speak with some of their clients to get a real sense of how they were guided to make good decisions during recessions or difficult times. Don't be afraid to ask them what they did with clients before, during, and after big market declines. If they claim that they sold their clients' investments before the last recession because they saw it coming, politely excuse yourself from the conversation. Your advisor cannot predict the timing or depth of recessions and market declines, but you should confidently ask them how they prepare clients for those tough times.

> Don't be afraid to ask potential advisors what they did with clients before, during, and after big market declines. A calm sea does not a good sailor make.

Ours plan for clients' money comes in the form of The Investment Strategy Guide®, which outlines the expectations and behaviors of both the advisor and the client in times of distress. It also shares the business plan for the money that's entrusted to us, our research process, how we select investments, and the purpose of the investment money. Whatever your advisor calls it, the point is that you should not leave those decisions to the moment of crisis. If you haven't written it out, agreed upon it, discussed it, committed to it, and signed a document about it, then you're not prepared to make hard decisions in times of high uncertainty.

In short, it's not a good idea to wait for the storm to decide what you're going to do in the storm.

KEY TAKEAWAYS

- Financial underperformance tends to result from one of two common emotions: fear or greed.
- Failure to control your fear and greed can have disastrous consequences, whereas sticking to a plan based on facts and analysis can lead to a truly stress-free relationship with money.
- Working with a level-headed, experienced fiduciary can help you get out of your own way, develop a rational plan, and stay the course through emergencies.

CONCLUSION

Recently, a referral came to us and said he'd had a conversation about the markets, the election, what's going on with China, and so on, with his golfing buddy. His golfing buddy, a client of ours had a simple reply: "I don't worry about that anymore. I've got it covered." In one way or another, that's the mindset you deserve. You've got to get to the point where you feel confidence and peace of mind with your financial life.

When you get these seven obstacles cleared out, are no longer swayed by greed or fear, understand the risk you're taking, know your financial strategy is appropriate to your goals, and don't hang on every financial fast food headline, you—like the relaxed golfer—will have a stress-free relationship with money. We aim for that outcome with every new client, and I wish it for you as well. I've watched people who've felt a financial burden for a decade or more stop worrying after a couple of meetings.

In my experience, reaching those clear numbers and having

full confidence in a plan requires professional assistance. If you read a medical journal or a newsletter from WebMD, would it ever give you so much confidence you'd decide to remove your own appendix? Of course not. Such surgery is very serious, and you'd want to trust an experienced professional with steady hands. Getting out of your own way means understanding which decisions can be made on your own and which ones require consulting a professional fiduciary.

Recognize what you know and what you don't know. Understand that you give yourself a much better chance of successful outcomes and a solid financial future if you at least consult with an objective expert in this industry. There's also collective wisdom in working with a fiduciary who has a variety of experiences and decades of experience with other people who've achieved what you're hoping for. The result is the ability to get quality advice, temper your emotions, stay the course through difficult times, say goodbye to your stress and worry, and say hello to a healthy, reassuring, sustainable relationship to your finances.

Positive change lies within reach. Go get it. If you'd like to have a conversation about how the principles and strategies in this book apply to you personally, please go to goalsconversation. com to schedule a time to talk.

ABOUT THE
AUTHOR

CHAD WILLARDSON, AWMA®, CRPC® is the president and founder of Pacific Capital, a fiduciary wealth advisory firm he started in 2011 after nine years of climbing the ranks as an investment advisor at Merrill Lynch. Currently, Chad also manages a

$350 million investment portfolio as the elected City Treasurer in his community. He created and trademarked The Financial Life Inspection®, a unique process to remove the stress people feel about their money. He's been featured in *The Wall Street Journal, Forbes, Inc., U.S. News & World Report, Investment News, Entrepreneur*, and *Financial Advisor*, and the bestselling book *Who Not How* by Dr. Benjamin Hardy, Tucker Max, and Dan Sullivan.

Chad is passionate about financial education and believes that with the right tools and resources, people can be empowered to make smart money decisions. As a Certified Financial Fiduciary, he loves to help people organize their financial life, clarify their goals, and make decisions that lead them to a successful and fulfilling life.

Outside of his business, Chad loves to travel. He served as a volunteer for two years on a church service mission in Lithuania, Latvia, Estonia, and Belarus and can speak, read, and write fluently in Lithuanian. Above all, Chad cherishes his family. A native of Orange County, California, Chad and his wife of nineteen years live in Corona with their five beautiful children.

Made in the USA
Monee, IL
09 June 2021